Don Aldinger
2532 Allentown Road
Quakertown, Pa. 18951
(215) 538-1817
Bought: 10/12/02

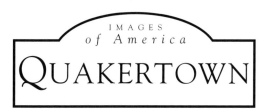

IMAGES
of America

QUAKERTOWN

D1599550

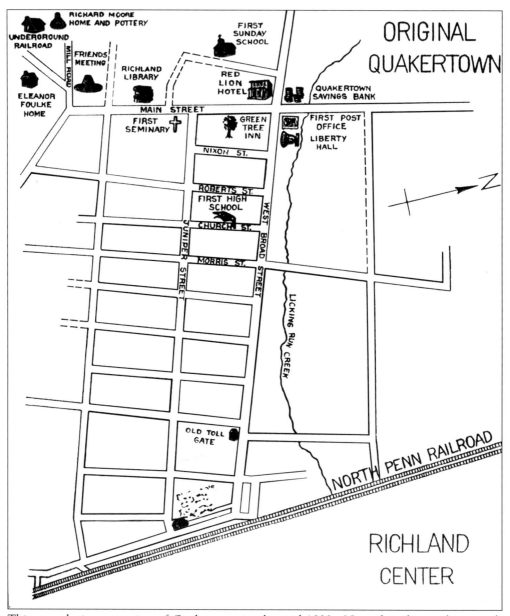

This map depicts a portion of Quakertown in the mid-1800s. Note that the south-to-north streets were not then numbered. For example, what is now Tenth Street was then Roberts Street.

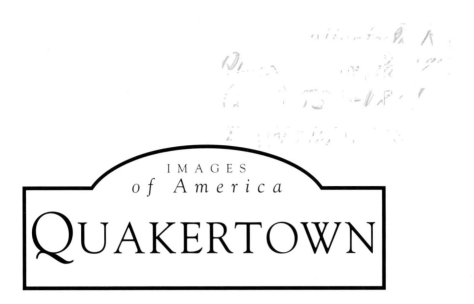

IMAGES
of America

QUAKERTOWN

Carolyn E. Potser, John T. Pilecki,
and Nancy Walp Bosworth

ARCADIA

Copyright © 2002 by Carolyn E. Potser, John T. Pilecki, and Nancy Walp Bosworth.
ISBN 0-7385-1099-8

First printed in 2002.

Published by Arcadia Publishing,
an imprint of Tempus Publishing, Inc.
2A Cumberland Street
Charleston, SC 29401

Printed in Great Britain.

Library of Congress Catalog Card Number: 2002108536

For all general information contact Arcadia Publishing at:
Telephone 843-853-2070
Fax 843-853-0044
E-Mail sales@arcadiapublishing.com

For customer service and orders:
Toll-Free 1-888-313-2665

Visit us on the internet at http://www.arcadiapublishing.com

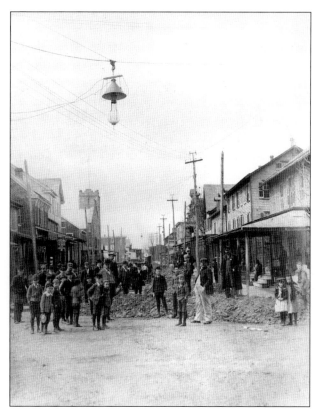

The photographer of this picture stood in the intersection of East Broad Street and Hellertown Avenue and aimed his camera west. Bystanders have been drawn to inspect progress on the new trolley tracks being installed on East Broad Street in 1896. The building left of center with the tower is the early Quakertown Transit Company trolley car barn, which was in use from 1896 to 1929.

CONTENTS

ACKNOWLEDGMENTS

This book was made possible through the combined efforts and leadership of three remarkable people—Carolyn Potser, John Pilecki, and Nancy Bosworth. Each brought a special gift to the project. For years, Nancy Bosworth has been archiving the materials, such as photographs and documents, collected by the Quakertown Historical Society. John Pilecki scanned hundreds of photographs, researched and wrote the education and sports chapters, and created the layout. Finally, Carolyn Potser wrote the introduction and 8 of the 10 chapters with a light touch that keeps the book interesting for the casual reader. Take away any one of these three and this project would never have been completed.

Of course, many other people worked very hard on this book too. A team of dedicated volunteers spent hours researching through the archives of the Quakertown Historical Society, personal collections, and the photographs brought in by people hoping to help the project. They include Lynda Ulrich, Jackie Mohr, Beryl Bosma, Calvin Ruth, Nancy and Don Roberts, Roger Lewis, Steve Biddle, and Nancy Janyszeski.

Many current and former residents brought their treasures to be included in this book. In no particular order, they are Bob Barndt, Don Young, Dave and Sue Wilsey, Jon Roberts, Gail DeReiter, Pat Edwards, Brenda Loux, Nancy Peters Ryan, Ray Fox, Ray and Betty Fulmer, Merv Afflerbach, Kenny Wieland, Bill Peischel, Arlington Lewis, Russ Schanley, Bill Harr, Shirley Neubert, Emilie Frankenfield, Rebecca Tuszynski, Renee Horne, Jane Renninger, David and Dorothea Weamer, Jackie Sine Brunner, Fay Fachet, Jon Biddle, Jim Rosch, the Knauss family, John Edge, Marjorie Brannaka, and Josephine Ahlum.

Finally, thanks must be given to people who helped with other aspects of this book. Dave Woglom and George Banas of the Quakertown Borough government contributed photographs from the borough's archive. Paul Schultz of the Quakertown American Legion Post No. 242 shared photographs and background material. George and Ray Fox checked the facts for the sports chapter and then wrote the introduction. Arlington Lewis also checked the sports chapter. Dr. Robert Leight helped write the education chapter. Dr. James Newcomer and Dr. James Scanlon encouraged the use of the Quakertown Community School District resources. Ann Hellman shared information about the Foulke family, and Ellen Schroy shared information about the Richland Library Company and the early Quakers. Tom Parrish and Quakertown Senior High School students Nick Loris and Erin Wimmer helped scan the photographs. The artwork of James Mann added to the spirit of this book. Finally, thanks are due to Jackie Mohr for all her typing. We regret anyone we missed.

—Pam Coleman
Certified Main Street Manager
Quakertown Alive!
www.quakertownalive.com

INTRODUCTION

In 1705, in a letter to William Penn, James Logan used the name "Great Swamp" to describe the large area that now includes Richland and Milford Townships and the borough of Quakertown. Not a swamp in the strict sense of the word, the territory nevertheless had many low areas, which required draining before they could be tilled. After 1720, the area gradually became known as "Rich Land," a term appropriate for its fertile soil. Richland had heavy stands of timber and abounded with wild animals. Tohickon and Swamp Creeks were rich in fish, and salt licks attracting wildlife gave Licking Run Creek its name. The Lenni Lenape Indians who lived along these creeks were a peaceable tribe.

Also peace loving were the first white settlers in Richland, English and Welsh Friends, popularly referred to as Quakers, who left their kindred in Gwynned, Montgomery County. Friends lived amicably with the American Indians, who were often helpful in supplying newcomers with provisions and in teaching them how to live in harmony with the environment. Peter Lester, the first settler in 1710, was soon followed by his son-in-law, John Ball, and by Hugh Foulke, second son of Edward and Eleanor Foulke who had settled in Gwynned in 1698. (Descendants of the Foulke family celebrated the family's 300th anniversary in America in 1998 and visited local landmarks.)

The first local gathering of Friends to seek God in a Quaker manner was held at the home of Peter Lester in 1710. To form a "Monthly Meeting," a gathering to conduct business, delegates from the Great Swamp went to Gwynned, the closest larger meeting. Permission was granted and guidance provided to establish a meetinghouse near the intersection of Old Bethlehem Pike and Station Road. This house, built of logs in 1716, was replaced in 1725 by another wooden structure on the site, now occupied by the present stone meetinghouse built in 1862.

In accordance with the Quaker method of doing business, overseers were appointed: John Ball and Hugh Foulke in 1730 and Abraham Griffith and William Edward in 1740. Minutes of Swamp Meetings give glimpses into some of the hardships and lives of its members, into their desire to preserve peace with the American Indians, and into their disapproval of slavery. Intrinsic to their silent worship was the principle of allowing God to speak to each worshiper. The present Friends of Richland Meeting maintain the same beliefs as the first to come to these rich lands and preserve the legacy of buildings and the grounds that early members created. An illustration of the strong Quaker emphasis upon learning was the establishment of the Richland Library Company in 1788, when local natives were still living in wigwams along Swamp Creek. Located at 44 South Main Street since 1911, the library contains many rare books and volumes of the original collection.

In the mid-1700s, the list of names kept by the tax collector included the German names of Landis, Klein, Clemmer, Musselman, and Yoder, along with the older Quaker names of Lester, Foulke, Ball, Jones, and Roberts. The German settlers established traditions that still influence community life. Soon after building their homes, they organized congregations and erected churches and schools. They excelled in music and introduced it into their churches. They were industrious and became hardworking farmers and craftsmen. During the Revolution, they were loyal to the American cause.

In 1734, the provincial court officially established the township of Richland. In the center of a plain in Richland lay what was to become the borough of Quakertown. Inevitably, a hamlet came into existence at the crossroads of two well-traveled roads, one leading from Bethlehem to Philadelphia and the other from Milford to the southern part of Bucks County. The public house of Walter McCool, at first called McCool's Tavern and later called the Red Lion Inn, was built at this crossroads in 1747. William Green built the first post office and store in 1803. Conditions of the roads were very poor. The highway leading east from the village was almost impassable except in the summer, and a dense forest lined both sides of the road. Consequently, the settlement called "Quakers Town" grew slowly, lining the sides of what was to become Main Street.

One of the most dramatic episodes in local history occurred when the Liberty Bell "slept" overnight on September 23, 1777, behind Liberty Hall, en route to its wartime hiding place in Allentown.

Of special interest to some historians is the Fries Rebellion of 1799. Led by Pennsylvania German farmers and named for one of its leaders, John Fries, the protest was the first armed resistance to the 1798 federal house tax. The rebellion represented an early challenge to the authority of the federal government and its power to tax.

With the arrival of the North Pennsylvania Railroad in 1856 came expansion and development. In a few years, the downtown became a busy village known as Richland Centre, which had its own post office in 1867. The road running east and west connecting the two villages was improved and named Broad Street, and the 12 intervening streets were given numbers for names. Quakertown was incorporated into a borough in 1855. Richland Centre was annexed to Quakertown in 1874.

Growth of the town was sustained by business and industry. Manufactured products included cigars, tools, boots, shoes, clothing, harnesses, spokes, handles, stoves, and church organs. The establishment of the Quakertown National Bank in 1877 facilitated business transactions. In 1881, the *Free Press* newspaper began serving businesses and individuals.

Social, educational, and religious institutions multiplied and strengthened, creating the town that Quakertown residents know today. The popular Quakertown Band was organized in 1877, and the volunteer fire companies have protected residents since 1882. A strong public school system continues to earn respect, and numerous churches have sprung up to serve this prospering community. Quakertown volunteers and community members continue to follow the example of the town's first settlers who understood the importance of working together.

—Carolyn E. Potser

One

WORSHIPING IN
OUR CHURCHES

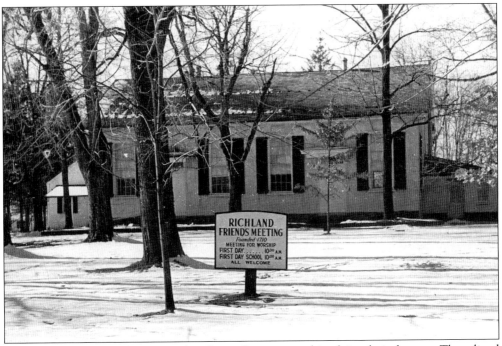

Until 1716, Quakers living in the Great Swamp worshiped in their homes. They lived peaceably with their American Indian neighbors while maintaining their simple life and strong belief that God is in everyone. They built their first meetinghouse of logs *c.* 1716 one mile south of the present site. That ground, however, was too rocky to serve as a burial ground, and in 1725, they relocated to the present 10-acre site, now bounded by South Main Street, Park Avenue, Route 309, and Mill Road. Their first meetinghouse in this location was also wooden, but in 1862, they built their present stone meetinghouse. An interesting historical anecdote sheds light on the Quaker principles of "silent worship in meeting" and "waiting upon the Spirit." Around 1769, a 12-year-old German boy named Jacob walked five miles with some of his Quaker friends to attend Richland Friends Meeting. On his return home, his father asked what had happened at the meeting. Jacob answered simply, "No one *said* anything, but God spoke to me all the way home." A walk through the grounds of Richland Friends Meeting under massive ancient trees lets one reflect upon these people who believe in "simplicity, silence, sincerity, and honoring each other's good deeds."

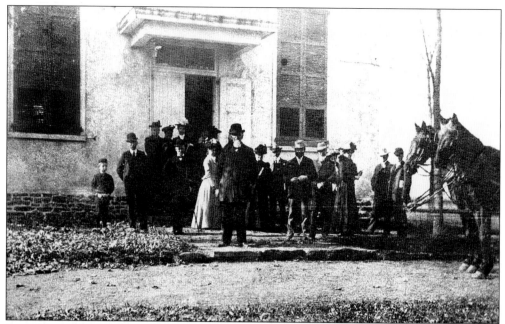

Preparing to depart following First Day worship, the Richland Friends gather in front of the entrance to their meetinghouse. This picture was probably taken in the late 1800s.

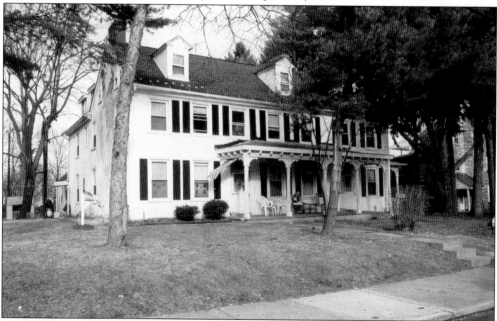

At this 1834 residence, 401 South Main Street, Quaker Richard Moore manufactured Redware pottery. At night, in wagons ordinarily used for shipping pottery, Moore hid runaway slaves and transported more than 600 of them north toward Canada. Since three major escape routes converged in Quakertown, it was a major station on the Underground Railroad despite the town's population of fewer than 200 residents. Moore's clandestine operation was a dramatic illustration of a Friend upholding an essential concept of his faith: a strong belief in the freedom and dignity of all persons regardless of color or creed.

10

In 1860, two Protestant groups, St. John's Lutheran and the Reformed, were organized. The two congregations united in the erection of this union church on Tenth Street in 1865. In 1870, the first pipe organ, a Durner instrument, was installed. In 1893, members dissolved their union arrangement and the Reformed members sold their share to the Lutherans for $300. In 1915, a new parsonage was built to serve the adjacent St. John's Lutheran Church.

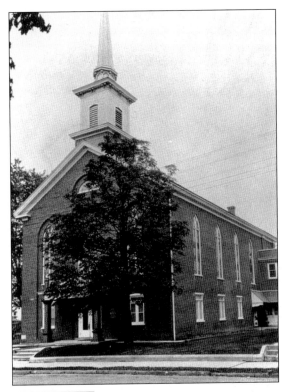

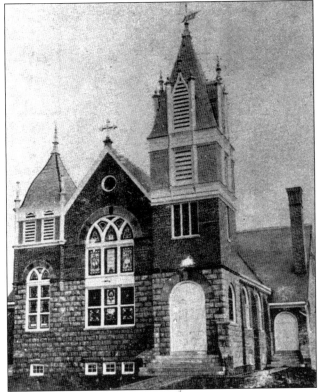

After separating from a union church arrangement in the period from 1869 to 1893 with St. John's Lutheran Church on Tenth Street, followers of the Reformed faith built this church on West Broad Street in 1894 and named it the First Reformed Church. Volunteer members did the work of excavating. In October 1961, the congregation celebrated its centennial. Needing more space for all church activities, the congregation, now involved in a merger with the Congregational Church and known as the United Church of Christ, built a new stone church in 1964 at Fourth Street and Park Avenue.

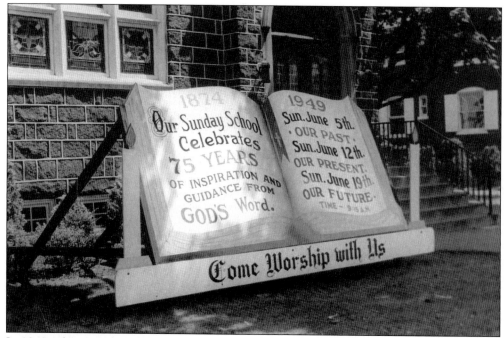

In 1949, a large signboard in front of the First Reformed Church, later named the First United Church of Christ, announced the 75th anniversary celebration of its Sunday school. The church building, now adapted to office use by professionals, is on West Broad Street near Fifth Street. Since 1964, the congregation has worshiped in a new building at Fourth Street and Park Avenue.

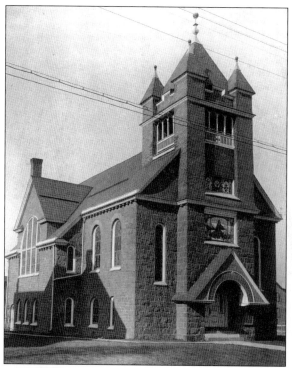

From its construction in 1893 to 1959, when it was closed, this church on the southwest corner of Erie and North Hellertown Avenues housed the Trinity Lutheran congregation. The congregation was organized c. 1881 by Rev. D.H. Reiter and originally met in Shive's Hall, on Front and Broad Streets, and in Citizens Hall. Since 1963, the Trinity Lutheran congregation has worshiped in its new church on the northwest corner of Erie and North Hellertown Avenues.

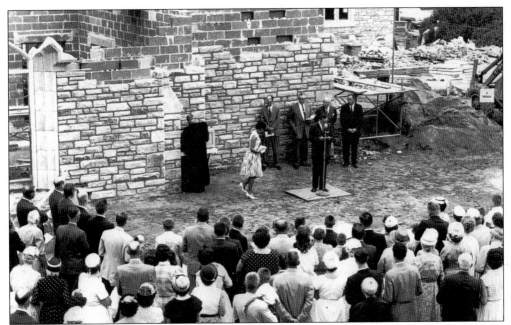

Clergy and laymen participated in the laying-of-the-cornerstone ceremony on June 24, 1962, for Trinity Lutheran Church, on Erie and North Hellertown Avenues. This church replaced the old one across the street, which was torn down. The education building remained behind the former church building.

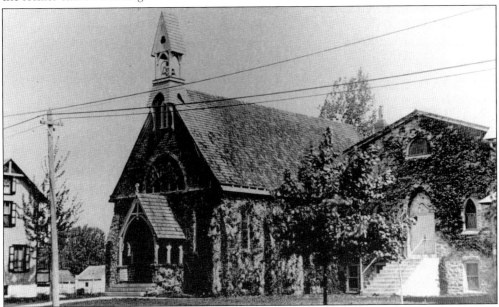

The original Emmanuel Episcopal Church on Broad and Fifth Streets was opened for divine worship in 1889. Contributions for its construction had come from churches in Philadelphia and its suburbs and from individuals in Philadelphia and the local community. The attached parish house was added in 1904. During Rev. Frederick Kettle's ministry, the Kinsey property at Ninth and Main Streets was bought and used to erect a new Episcopal church in 1964. Kettle ministered 22 years, the longest ministry in the church's history.

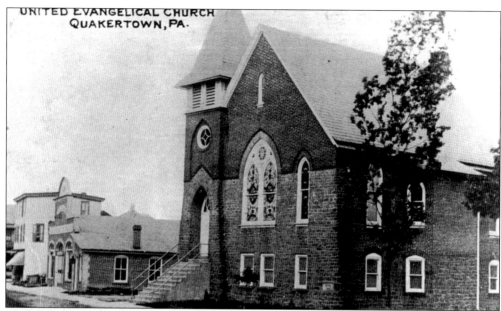

The United Evangelical Church on West Broad Street, formerly known as Branch Street, was built during the pastorate of George W. Hangen in 1897. A parsonage was built next to it a few years later. The church was destroyed by fire on February 7, 1947. The congregation bought the Clymer property on Eighth Street and converted it into a house of worship. In 1968, the United Evangelical Church merged with the Methodist Church, forming the United Methodist Church. Today, the Quakertown United Methodist Church occupies a new building on Frier Road.

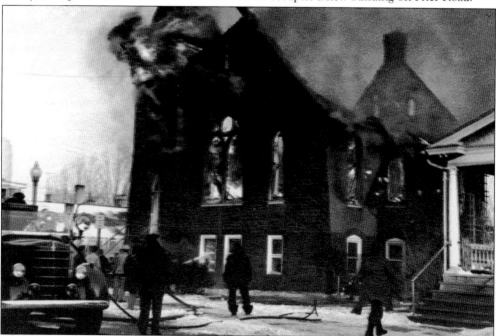

On Sunday morning, February 7, 1947, residents were shocked to witness the fire that devastated United Evangelical Church on West Broad Street, then Branch Street. The congregation relocated its church in a building on Eighth Street.

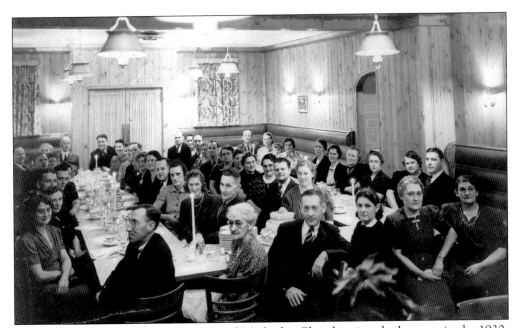

The Triple Link Bible Class of the United Methodist Church enjoyed a banquet in the 1930s at Trainer's Restaurant. Seated in the front row are, from left to right, Mr. and Mrs. A.D. Lawrence; Paul Dietz, president; Mary Dietz; Katie Dietz; and Alice Bush. Seated two persons behind Paul Dietz is Leonard White, well known for his interest in Quakertown's history.

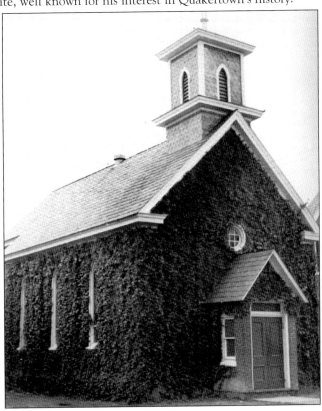

Underneath the ivy is Quakertown's first Catholic church, founded by Fr. Henry Stommel, dedicated on August 2, 1886, and named St. Isidore of Madrid after Isidore, the patron of farmers. Located on West Broad Street at Sixth Street, the church was constructed of brick by a Quakertown firm and featured a steeple, eight stained-glass windows, and a bell.

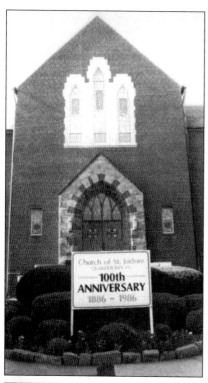

St. Isidore's Roman Catholic Church, on West Broad Street, was dedicated on January 9, 1953, replacing the small ivy-covered church built in 1886. The church celebrated its 100th anniversary in 1986.

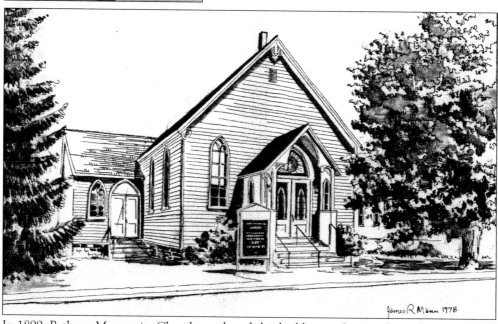

In 1899, Bethany Mennonite Church purchased this building on Juniper Street between Third and Fourth Streets, depicted in this drawing by James Mann, from Bethel United Methodist Church and formed a union with East Swamp, West Swamp, and Finland Mennonites. A.B. Shelly served as pastor for all four congregations. Between 1921 and 1969, the other groups withdrew and established their own churches. In 1979, Bethany joined with Flatland Mennonite Church on Erie Road. The merged group took the name United Mennonite Church.

Two
EDUCATING OUR YOUTH

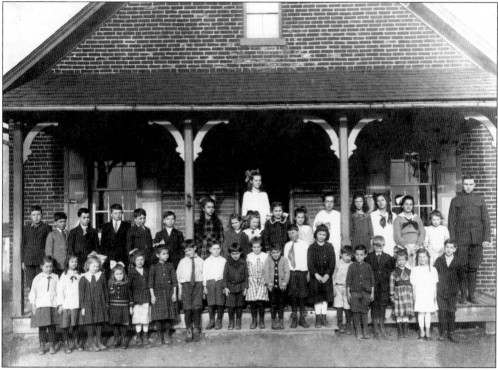

In 1834, Pennsylvania passed the Free School Act. Two decades later, the public schools were strengthened when the office of county schools superintendent was established to provide a "free public education" for the children in Bucks County. In response to this mandate, many one-room and multiroom schoolhouses were built over a wide area of upper Bucks County. Six separate school districts evolved within the area: Milford Township, the borough of Richlandtown, Richland Township, Haycock Township, the borough of Trumbauersville, and the borough of Quakertown. Typically, all these districts taught students from first through eighth grade. Richlandtown did maintain its own high school program until 1927, when it joined the other districts and sent its older students to the Quakertown School District, which had maintained a secondary curriculum since 1883. Many of the surrounding districts maintained their own elementary schoolhouses and curriculums until the early 1950s, when consolidation was completed and the Quakertown School District was formed. One such school is shown in this 1919 photograph—the Central School on Station Road in Richland Township. Because of the range in grades and ages within his class of 36 students, it can be assumed that the teacher, Franklin Slifer, was an early practitioner of such modern teaching methods as peer tutoring and small group instruction.

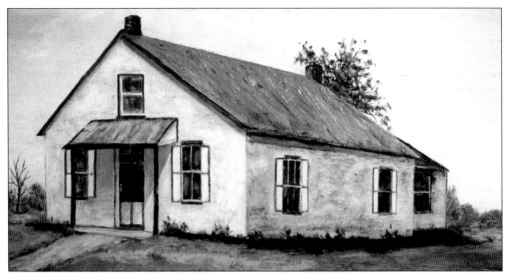

This painting by artist Calvin Ruth depicts the first schoolhouse built in the borough of Quakertown after its incorporation in 1855. The building was on the west side of what is now Fourteenth Street. A "public examination" of pupils was held on October 4, 1861. The performing students were Anna A. Van Houten, Angeline Hill, Dianna Strunk, Susan Grier, Edwin Ball, and James Shive. Mr. Foulke was their teacher. The building was razed in the 1960s.

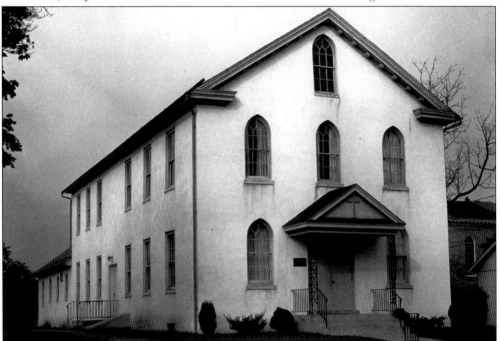

This more substantial building was built on Tenth Street in the 1880s. It served both elementary and secondary students. The high school program, established largely through the efforts of Rev. George Lazarus, pastor of St. John's Lutheran Church, occupied one room of the building. In 1884, these students received the first diplomas from Quakertown High School: Henrietta Mood, Carrie Ozias, and Samuel Berger. The Tenth Street building is currently in use by the United Friends School.

18

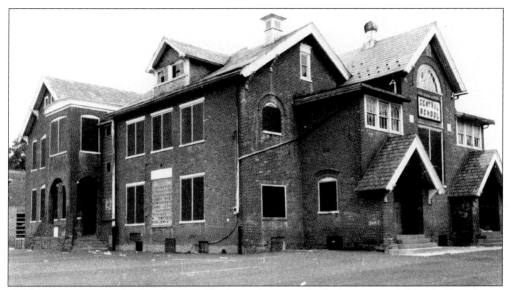

Quakertown's Central School, on Sixth Street between Park Avenue and Juniper Street, was built in 1880. Used at first for elementary students, the original structure was added to in 1892, and the older students moved from the Tenth Street building to the new addition at Central School. To meet the needs of increasing numbers of borough and neighboring district students who were extending their educations beyond eighth grade, two other additions were built in piecemeal fashion in the early 20th century.

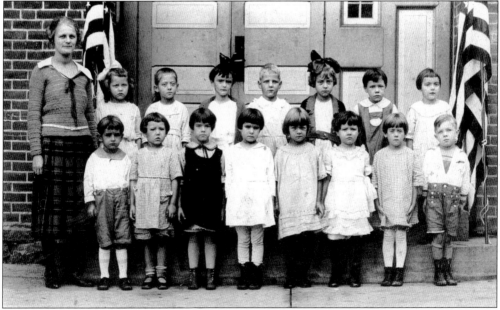

This group of 1922–1923 Central School kindergarten students attended class on the first floor of the building. Secondary students were educated on the second floor. Miss Kimposts is pictured here with her class. Included in the front row are Billy Moyer, Leanna Wenhold, Robert Wilson, Pinky ?, James Hanselman, Marjorie Diehl, and Billy Schissler. Standing in the back row are, from left to right, Pauline Achey, Edith Gehman, Marion Wenhold, Alfred Clifford Edge, Dorothy Ott, Kathleen Harr, and Peggy Hersh.

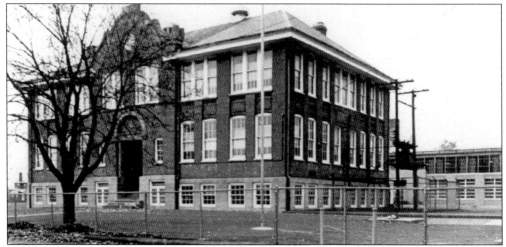

In 1911, another red schoolhouse, the Lincoln School, was erected next to the Central School. The second floor was first used for 11th- and 12th-grade classes, the first floor for offices and primary classes. In 1922, a six-year junior-senior high school program was created, and the second floors of the adjoining schools were reorganized. The Central School became the senior high, teaching grades 10 through 12, and the Lincoln School became the junior high, grades 7 through 9. Both first floors continued to house elementary classrooms.

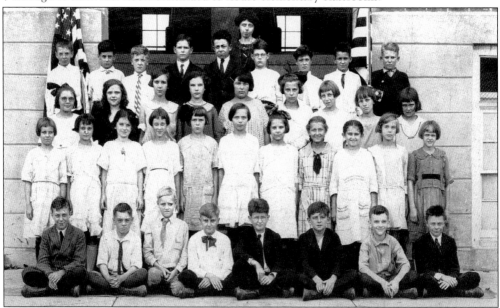

Students in Addie Moyer's 1922–1923 sixth-grade class pose in front of the Lincoln School. From left to right are the following: (first row) Edwin Eisenhart, Wilmer Moyer, Frederick Abenschein, Wayne Steeley, Ernest Hendricks, Jesse Landis, Lovine Deily, and Fred Ort; (second row) Hazel Smoll, Dorothy Fly, Kathryn Reider, Mildred Neubert, Ernadine Ambler, Marian Afflerbach, Helen Frederick, Jeanette Brown, Dorothy McColly, Evelyn Gammon, and Blanche Martin; (third row) Edna Shaddinger, Natalie Weikel, Lucille Ackerman, Katherine Althouse, Esther Fretz, Mary Kile, Helen Smoll, Jessie Weikel, and Pauline Auer; (fourth row) Albion Yoder, Max Cummings, Ken Fowl, Walter Steltzer, Jesse Painter, Paul Snyder, Walter Purcell, Oswald Smith, and Alonzo Courtney.

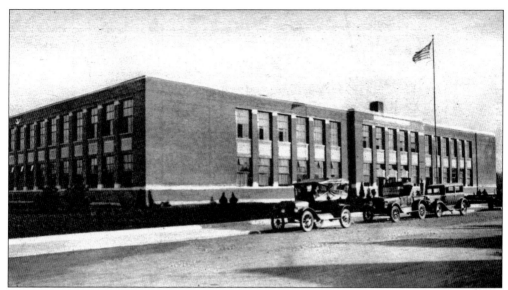

In 1927, the Department of Public Instruction issued a report that was highly critical of the conditions found in the Lincoln and Central buildings. The report cited "haphazard illumination," "offensive odors that penetrate into the building from the toilet rooms," and "outside pumps that are used for drinking water" as items that "fail to measure up to modern standards." In response, a modern junior-senior high school was built on Seventh Street near Park Avenue. The school opened in 1929 with the slogan "Enter to Learn, Leave to Serve" over the front doors.

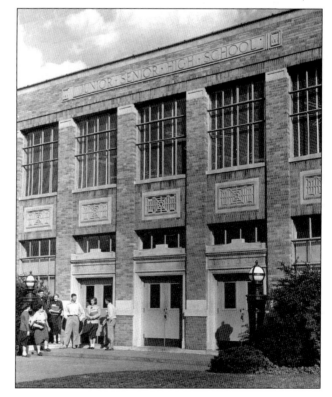

Students stand in front of the junior-senior high school shortly after its opening. The building was used for grades 7 through 12 from 1929 to 1955. The Central and Lincoln buildings continued to function as elementary schools and were also used by secondary students when the junior-senior high became overcrowded in the 1950s.

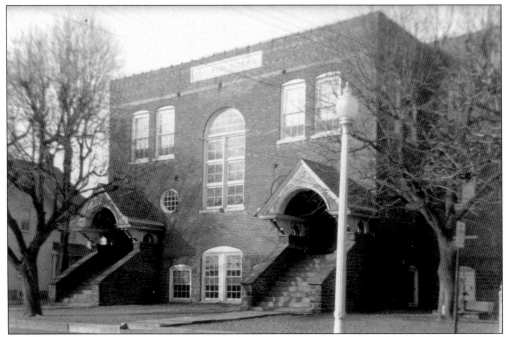

In the late 1800s, a school was built that would be used exclusively for elementary students for most of its history. This building, known as the Franklin School, was on the east side of the railroad tracks that run through the borough, in a section of town known originally as Richland Centre. The Franklin School served elementary students in this neighborhood until the Neidig School opened in 1958.

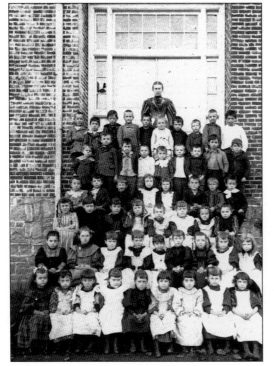

A proud teacher, Elmira Ochs, stands with her class of 53 students on the steps of the Franklin School in 1895. Ochs, herself an 1888 graduate of Quakertown High School, the school's fifth graduating class, can also be seen in the sports chapter of this book as a member of the Crescent Hill Tennis Club.

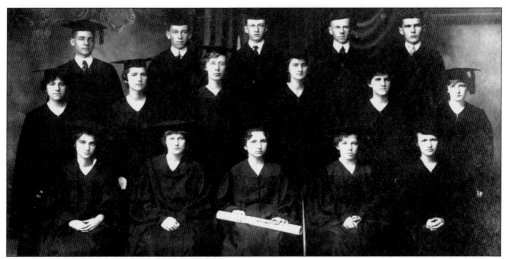

Members of the Class of 1917 pose for their graduation picture. They are, from left to right, as follows: (front row) Bella Cohen, Margaret Scheetz Moyer, Fannie Clymer, Ethel Price Stoneback, and Viola Longacre; (middle row) Laura Heimbach, Ruth Savitz, Mary Reissler, Margaret Ozias Scheetz, Elizabeth Moyer, and Vera Hartzell; (back row) Burtine Schanely, Paul Shelly, Clarence Johnson, Oliver King, and Jesse Cressman. Jesse Cressman went on to serve for many years as teacher and athletic director. A plaque on the Alumni Field bleachers honors his dedication.

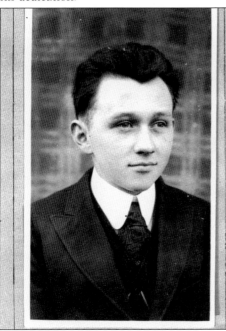

ALFRED S. JOHNSON

President of Senior Class; President of Literary Society; President of Athletic Association; Advertising Manager of "Little Quaker"; 1st Prize in Liberty Bond Oratorical Contest.

"Alf", "Dolly".

"Ain't love a peculiar thing."

We now have before us "Alf," who hails from Johnson's Corner. You never find him grouchy or his temper disturbed. His smile is as natural as his appetite and his quaint but ready wit have won for him the hearts of his classmates. His highest ambition is to own a garage, but we're sure he won't forsake farming altogether, especially the cultivating of "Biehns."

Alfred S. Johnson, the president of the Quakertown High School Class of 1920, would go on to become a prominent local businessman and community leader. His senior page in *Les Memories*, the predecessor to *Recall*, which is the Quakertown High School yearbook, proved to be quite accurate in its prediction for Alfred. He went on to co-own an automobile dealership and garage, and he "cultivated" classmate Mildred Biehn for marriage, who accepted and became his lifelong mate.

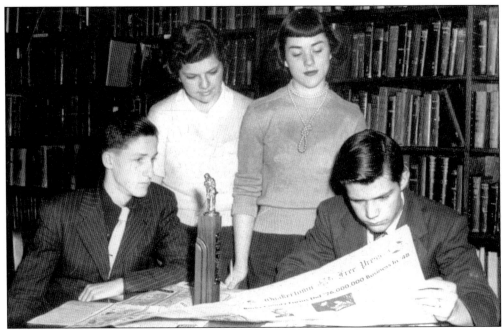

The sports editors of the 1949 *Recall* scan the *Free Press* for scores and other details to include in their yearbook articles. They are, from left to right, Jim Smith, Jessica Heimbach, Kathryn Weber, and Jim Rosch. Jim would go on to become a faithful supporter of Quakertown High School sports. He edited the football roster programs for all home games from 1966 to 1992.

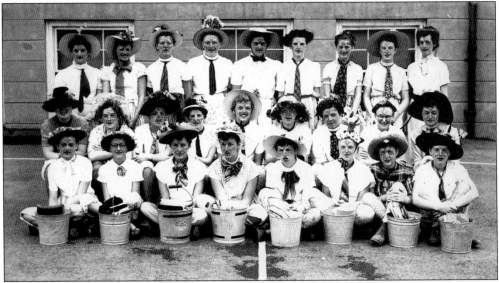

It is 1950, and the Commercial Club is putting its prospective members through the initiation grind. The pledges are, from left to right, as follows: (front row) Mary Price, Marian Minarik, Betty Troutman, Mary Lou Setman, Lorraine Loughridge, Dorothy Grant, Mary Ellen Koder, and Barbara Bergman; (middle row) Dorothy Gombert, Lorraine Gerhart, Mildred Moose, Lillian Simitz, Vivian Mease, Gloria Deose, Constance Jett, Teresa Swierzewska, and Lyra Shaffer; (back row) Suzanna Ross, Wilma Hartman, June Heavener, Ruth Hudson, Mildred Geissinger, Shirley Wimmer, Dorothy Snyder, Betty Rothmund, and Margaret Filburn.

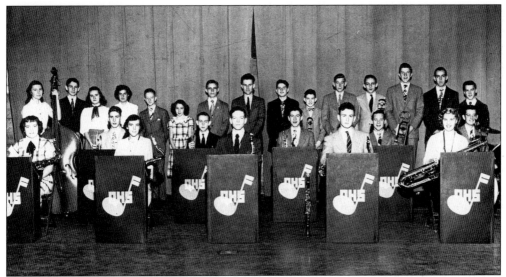

The Dance Band was a "versatile group of music makers," according to the 1949 *Recall*. From left to right are the following: (front row) J. Ginder, C. Tuttle, W. Long, R. Van Auken, and M. Fischer; (middle row) L. Betz, Z. Stauffer, E. Gaugler, R. Baird, and W. Meyers; (back row) L. Reese, R. VanAuken, J. Koons, C. Cygan, L. Fenstermacher, D. Strauss, J. Fulmer, ? Kunkle, D. Bush, H. Horne, C. Shelly, E. Afflerbach, W. Shelly, E. Weisner, and K. Mitchell.

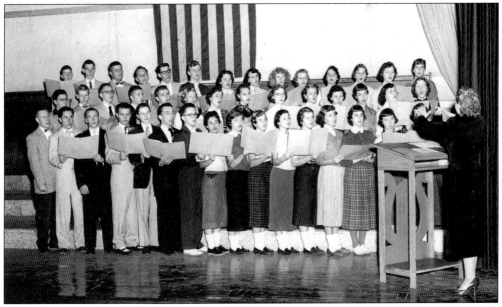

Henrietta Landis Jahnsen leads the 1955–1956 Quakertown High School Mixed Chorus. These seniors are, from left to right, as follows: (front row) H. Dietz, D. Newman, O. Mastin, K. Newman, K. Schultz, R. Cole, R. Kistler, J. Griffo, N. Stein, M. Pfaff, R. Holsinger, S. Gehringer, R. Willauer, J. Lacey, N. Cunningham, and F. Salvaggio; (middle row) A. Schmeck, G. McCurdy, L. Erwin, D. Moyer, C. Texter, L. Leinbach, H. Stout, B. Butler, R. Renninger, A. Minarik, J. Awckland, J. Angstadt, N. Moyer, and J. Kummerer; (back row) D. Nace, T. Bozarth, R. Richmond, R. Boardman, T. Mumbauer, A. Schneider, S. Moyer, D. Brunner, B. Sabulis, P. Shelly, P. Stumb, D. Horne, C. Forry, and E. Trauger.

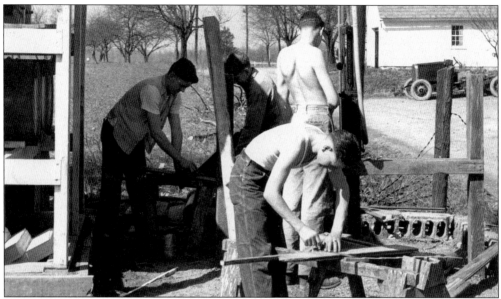

These industrious students are enrolled in the Quakertown High School agricultural course, an important part of the school's vocational program for many years. Those who chose this course of studies worked on the Quakertown High School farm on California Road, near the site of the YMCA indoor tennis facility. Students from neighboring districts such as Sell-Perk also attended this farm school. The students participated in many extracurricular activities, including sports competition in the regional Future Farmers of America league, and earned numerous honors, as when Willard Doctor was awarded the Star Farmer of Pennsylvania title in 1950.

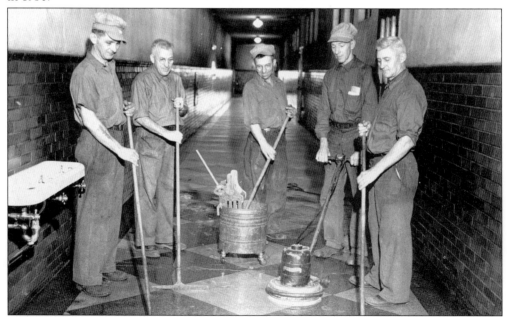

During the early 1950s, these hardworking men kept the floors in the hallways of the junior-senior high school on Seventh Street sparkling clean. They are, from left to right, Ralph Stahr, Leidy Lewis, Wilson Scheetz, Calvin Ruth Sr., and Charles Kline.

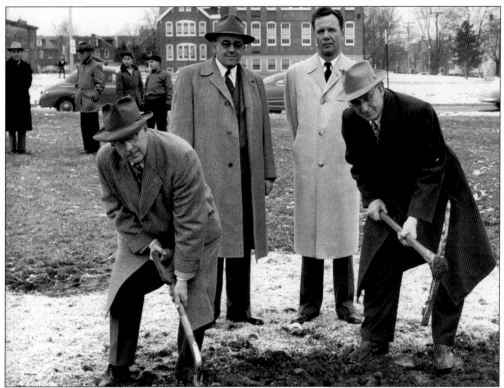

The groundbreaking ceremony for the new Quakertown Senior High School at 600 Park Avenue was conducted in 1955 by, from left to right, Cooper Smith, general contractor; Joseph S. Neidig, superintendent of the Quakertown School District; George Scholes, chief burgess; and Lyman Koehler, school board president. Note the buildings behind the participants. On the north side of Park Avenue are the Central School, on the left, and the Lincoln School, on the right. These buildings were razed in the 1970s.

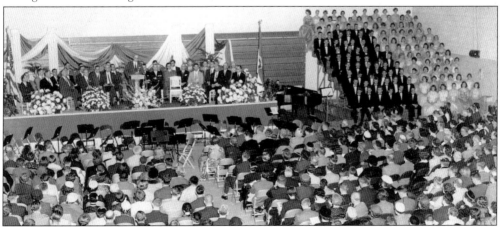

On Thursday, December 13, 1956, some 950 people gathered in the gymnasium of the new Quakertown Senior High School and heard Charles H. Boehm, longtime Bucks County superintendent of schools, dedicate the new building. The senior high mixed chorus sang *The Dedicatory Hymn*, *Hallelujah* from Handel's *Messiah*, and the alma mater. The senior high band also performed.

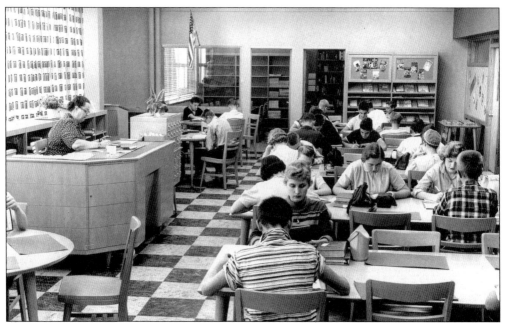

Generations of Quakertown High School students remember the tight ship run by school librarian Elizabeth Treffinger at both the high school on Seventh Street and the facilities of the Park Avenue building, pictured here. A new library and a new gymnasium were added to the Park Avenue building in 1988, and the original library was converted to classroom space.

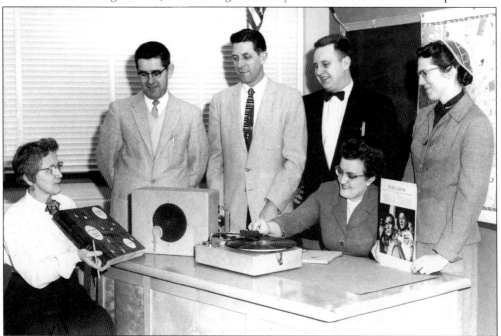

In this 1950s photograph, the Quakertown High School English department reviews a recording of *Julius Caesar*, perhaps to supplement their instruction of the classic play. The instructors, who are exploring new methods of teaching the Bard, are, from left to right, Miss Stever (department head), Mr. Boomhower, Mr. Wisneski, Mr. Schrader, Miss Potser, and Miss Bergey.

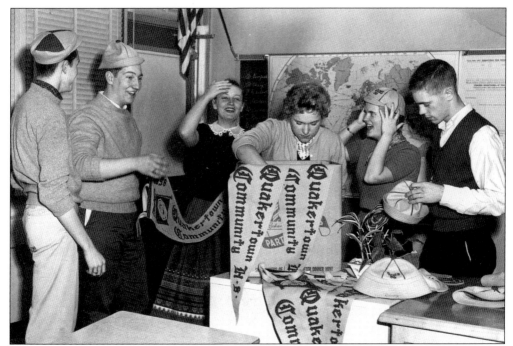

Members of the Class of 1958 check out their pennants and beanies, which at one time were sold to each member of the incoming sophomore class. These excited sophomores would be among the second class to graduate from the new high school. They are, from left to right, Fred Dunlap, Bruce Dennis, Gail Andrews, Baiba Dale, Lois Wackerman, and Roger Moyer.

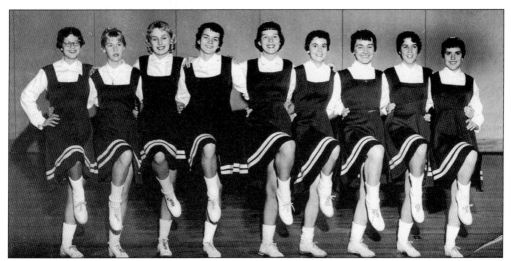

These sharp-looking Quakertown High School cheerleaders in 1958 are, from left to right, Janet Thornton, Carol Witmer, Linda Farrell, Susan Scully, Nancy Wyckoff, June Leister, Ruth Stumb, Diane Cummings, and Shirley Pearson.

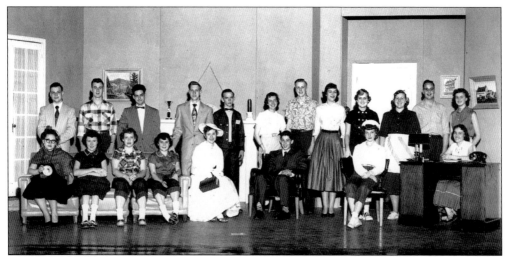

"Assuming imaginary roles, class thespians presented the unforgettable *Quiet Summer*." That is how the 1954 *Recall* described the junior play of that year. The cast members are, from left to right, as follows: (front row, sitting) N. Balodis, J. Walker, J. Harner, S. Luma, P. Kepner, J. Leister, J. Springer, and P. Repash; (back row, standing) G. Stump, R. Hilmer, R. Zakeosian, R. Schmidt, G. Gerhart, R. Hunsberger, W. Schuetz, M. Smith, S. Trauger, A. Yeakel, J. Adams, and F. Sell.

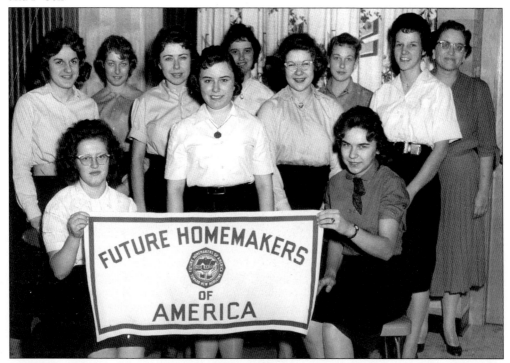

The Future Homemakers of America Club was an organization that allowed female students to give service to the high school through skills learned in their home economics classes. From left to right are the following: (front row) M. Baringer, N. Walp, and M. Freed; (middle row) E. Hinkle, L. Hoch, B. Roeder, and B. Benner; (back row) L. Harner, J. Fox, V. Althouse, and advisor Helen McSparrin.

Three

ESTABLISHING
TRANSPORTATION

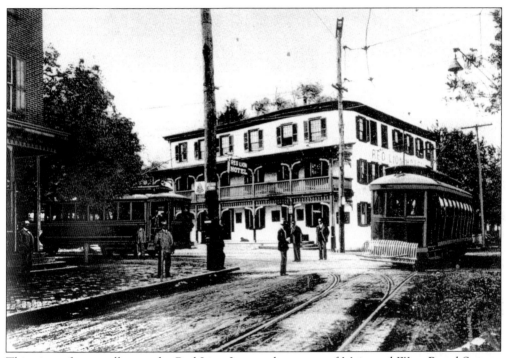

This view of two trolleys at the Red Lion Inn, at the corner of Main and West Broad Streets, recalls the early years of the 20th century, when both the *Liberty Bell* and the *Tripper* hummed along the streets of town. There was probably much truth in the lines "I bring new life and faces to old sleeping towns and places / and a million homes are brighter for the music of my song," from *Song of the Trolley*, by Roy L. McCardell. If this picture were in color, we could see the bright red body of the *Liberty Bell* as it travels south on Main Street, following the route of Old Bethlehem Pike on its journey from Allentown to Philadelphia, and the striped red-and-white *Tripper* as it rounds the corner on its hourly run between Quakertown and Richlandtown. Of the 200 electric trolleys operated by the Lehigh Valley Transit Company between 1903 and 1951, which locals dubbed the *Liberty Bell*, only three have been saved for museums. Car 1030, with the placard "Philadelphia Express," is displayed at the Seashore Trolley Museum in Kennebunkport, Maine. None of the 10 cars that were owned by the Quakertown Traction Company remained.

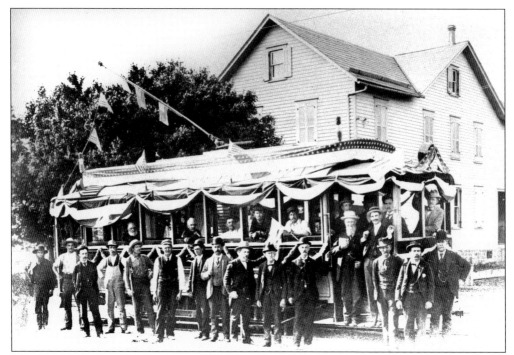

This first trolley car in Quakertown was one of 10 operated by the Quakertown Traction Company chartered in 1896. The trolleys were housed in the company's powerhouse and trolley barn on East Broad Street. Nicknamed the *Tripper*, the trolley followed a route that began at Main and West Broad, went down Broad, turned north on Third, turned right and crossed a bridge over the railroad tracks, came out Belmont Avenue to East Broad, to Hellertown Avenue and Tohickon Avenue, and crossed the Tohickon bridge on its way to Richlandtown.

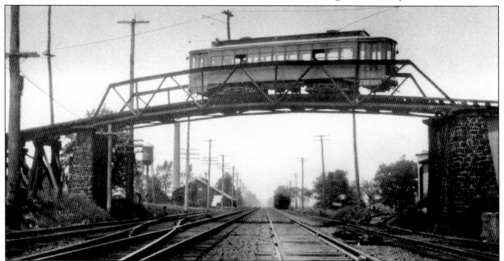

The iron trolley bridge that crossed the railroad tracks behind the Palace Theatre and the Globe Hotel, 100 yards north of the railroad station, was a local wonder. Older residents recall that children hung on tightly while the *Tripper* crossed over the steeply graded bridge, afraid that the trolley would jump the tracks. In 1935, the bridge was removed in two sections by the railroad's wrecker between the passing of trains.

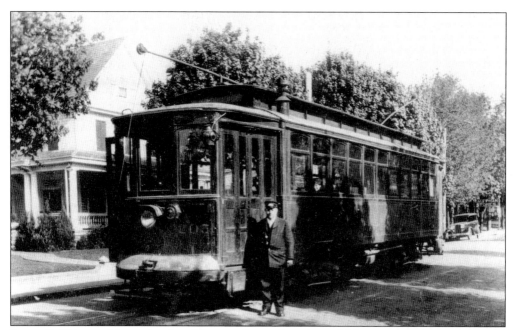

Farewell, *Tripper*. After more than 30 years of providing dependable service and entertainment, the *Tripper* retired in June 1929. Conductor John Bean might have been thinking wistfully of driving *Tripper* number five, the "summer car," decked out in colored electric lights and curtains for Gay Nineties excursions. Trolley parties were popular, and clubs chartered a car for an evening of merriment. Or maybe Bean was remembering those exciting times when firemen were allowed to attach their wagons to the back of the trolleys.

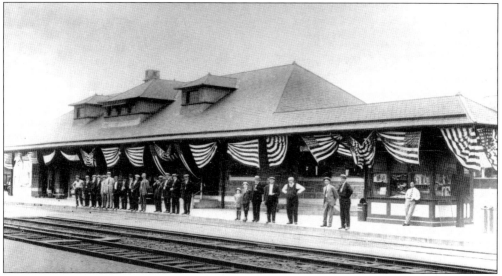

Men and boys stand trackside at the train station to greet visitors *c.* 1914 for the town's weeklong Chautauqua Festival, a nationwide program of community-based public lectures, music, and theatrical performances. Built in 1902, the station was gutted by arson in 1989. More than a decade of community fundraising led to a $1 million restoration plan set for 2003. A fine example of Romanesque revival architecture, the station was awarded a listing on the National Register of Historic Places.

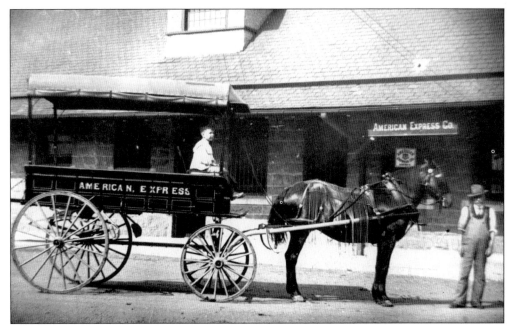

Pausing in front of the Quakertown Railroad Station *c.* 1915 and sitting on an American Express baggage wagon is Marshall Roberts, driving "Freddie Horse." Standing is Marshall's grandfather Andrew Jackson Roberts, the first Railway Express agent at the station. Andrew was the father of Clinton Roberts.

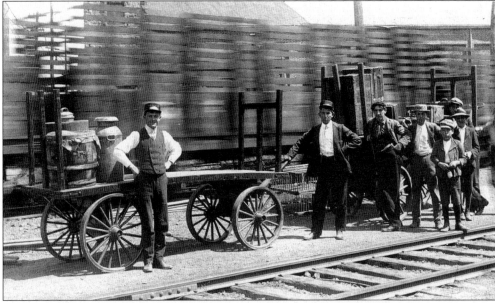

Dozens of daily passengers and freight trains, as well as trolleys, served the booming downtown at the beginning of the 20th century in the days before America fell in love with chrome and horsepower. To the left is Railway Express agent Clinton Roberts, the second of three generations of the Roberts family, who handled worldwide freight shipments entering or leaving town. In the center is baggage agent Connie Conway. The blur behind them is perhaps a slow-moving grain wagon.

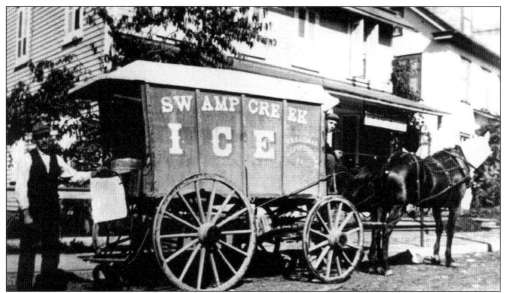

The iceman cometh! H.G. Hallman waves his merchandise during his daily rounds in this 1905 picture. Blocks were cut to fit into everyone's icebox, a crude double-walled appliance resembling a chest of drawers. It might preserve raw milk and meat for a few days, provided the children did not leave the door open. The economy of horse-drawn delivery favored local products over those of interstate commerce. In a nearby town, it is still said that Swamp Creek water is truly the purest.

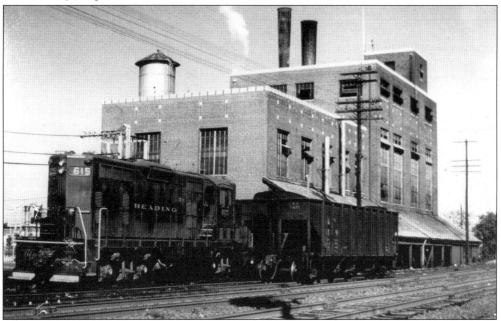

For decades, boiler coal to power steam turbines was delivered at trackside to the borough's electric generating plant until the plant closed in 1971. A Reading Railroad GP7, a heavy diesel locomotive, is pictured guiding the coal hopper car. In exchange for the closing, the borough gained a coveted wholesale power license, which has kept our retail rates among the state's lowest.

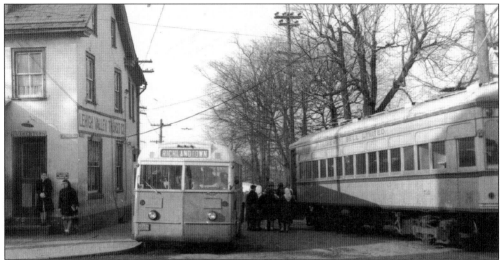

Illustrated at this transit hub at Main and West Broad Streets is the gradual progression of vehicles from electric trolley cars to gasoline buses. In the center is a Levy Company bus headed for Richlandtown. To the right, a Lehigh Valley Transit trolley, *Liberty Bell Limited*, heads north to Allentown. The building on the corner, used as a ticket office for many years, has served a variety of purposes, including an early bank.

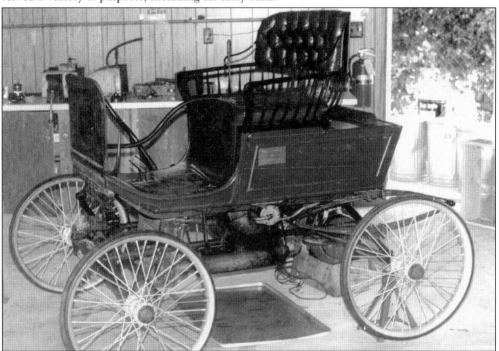

This classy car is a 1902 gasoline runabout built by John Nicholas, owner of the Nicholas Buggy and Carriage Company, on Juniper and Green Streets. The driver "worked the sparks" by hand, hoisted himself up onto the stirrup-like, floral-engraved "feet," and then clutched the metal tiller rod, not a wheel. Directly underneath the handsome red upholstered seat was the battery. Both the water tank and oil dripper were made of wood. The car is owned by the Quakertown Historical Society and is on display in the Market Place Barn on North Main Street.

Four

EARNING A LIVING

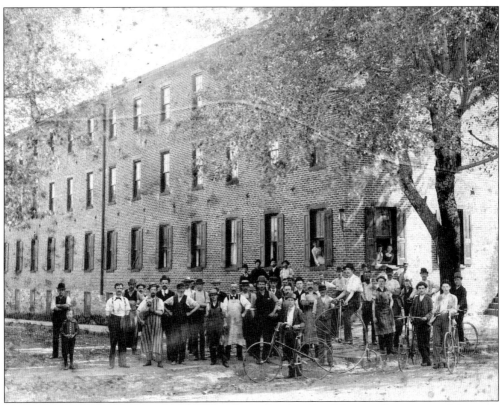

These leather workers have assembled outside the Quaker City Harness Company, at Main and Juniper Streets, possibly at the end of a long working day. In 1878, their employer, Jonas Harley, came to town and began the Quaker City Harness Company in a building beside the Red Lion Inn. In 1881, he moved his business to the former Continental Hotel at Main and Juniper Streets. He demolished this building in 1886 and built the large new three-story brick factory pictured here. Harley's company became one of the largest harness works in the country. He employed more than 140 skilled workers, who manufactured horse harnesses, reins, halters, saddles, and fly nets. In preparing the leather, workers immersed it in vats of grease and rubbed the hide by hand until it became supple and soft. When it was clean and pliable, it was dried, then cut into strips for harnesses and fly nets. Workers labored 10 hours a day plus 5 hours on Saturday, for which they received $9.50 a week. It was a successful business until the automobile became popular. Ironically, it was either Jonas Harley, or his son Fred Harley, who owned the first automobile in town in 1899.

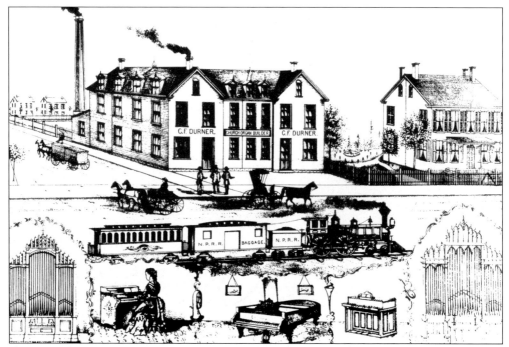

Pictured are the factory and residence of Charles E. Durner (1863–1932) at the northwest corner of Front and Juniper Streets, built during the 1860s. The Durner family engaged in the manufacture of church and parlor organs for five generations prior to relocating in town, and their products were among the finest available. A Durner pipe organ won the highest honors at the 1876 Centennial Exhibition in Philadelphia.

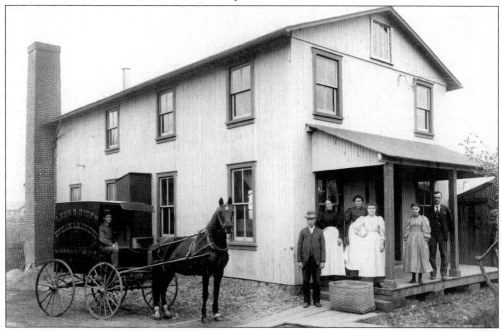

The delivery wagon for the William Loux and Harry H. Biehn (Bean) Steam Laundry stands next to the laundry building at 115 South Second Street in 1894. The laundry opened in 1893.

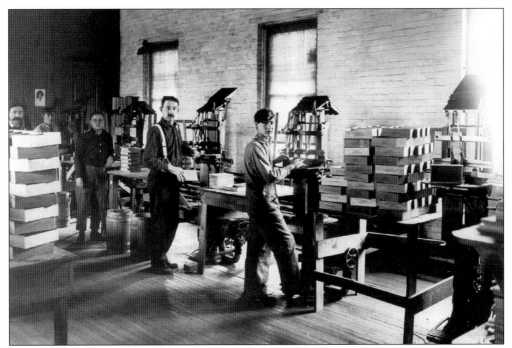

These unidentified cigar factory workers have paused in their work of rolling cigars to glance at the cameraman. At its height in the late 1800s and early 1900s, the cigar-making industry flourished in Quakertown.

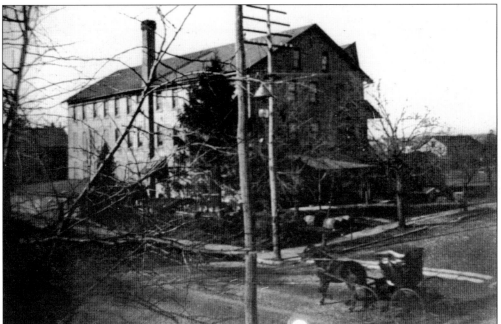

One of the foremost cigar manufacturers in town was Henry Sommer, who built a business that progressed from more than 100 family-style, or cottage, industries to a large cigar factory, this one at Tenth and Juniper Streets. Considered a pioneer in the cigar business, Henry Sommer produced 10.5 million cigars in 1887.

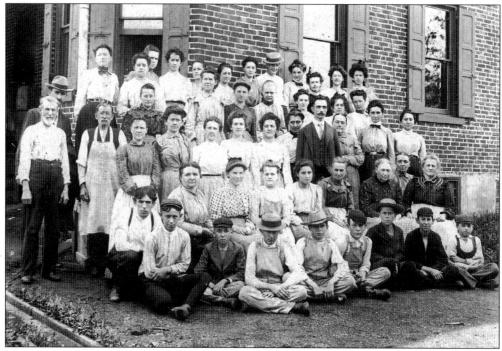

These cigar factory workers are gathered outside Henry Sommer's cigar factory at Tenth and Juniper Streets in 1899. This cigar-producing company was in business from 1867 to 1937.

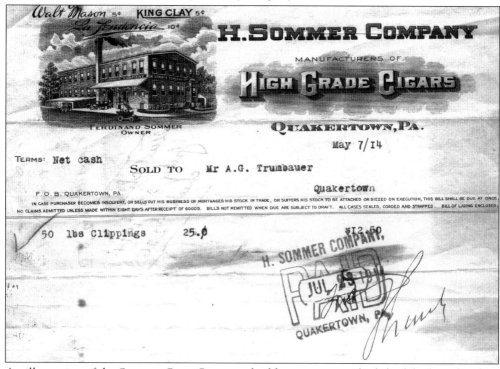

An illustration of the Sommer Cigar Company building appears to the left of the letterhead on this sales receipt for tobacco sold to A.G. Trumbauer in 1914.

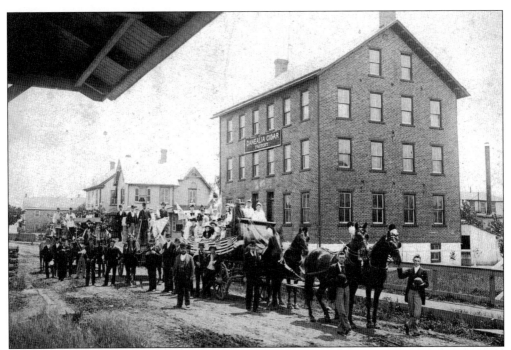

In this brick building at South Front Street and Park Avenue, cigar manufacturing was conducted first by William Suelke, then by Suelke and Bedford, and lastly by Ferdinand Sommer. Later, it was owned by the K & L Lumber Company. The little parade in the foreground may be a wedding procession.

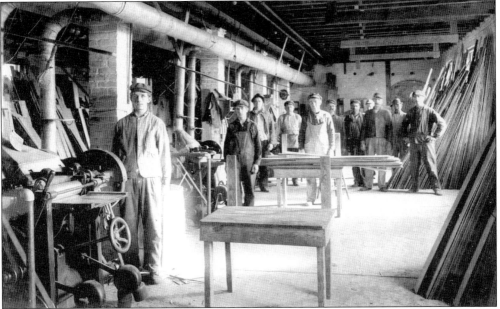

Workers pose inside the Keystone Box Company in the third ward. With cigar making the major local industry for almost a century, the manufacture of cigar boxes was a strong industry until the 1940s. The boxes were made of soft wood, lids were attached with fabric hinges, and the entire box was covered with ornate paper. Each box was unique for each brand of cigar.

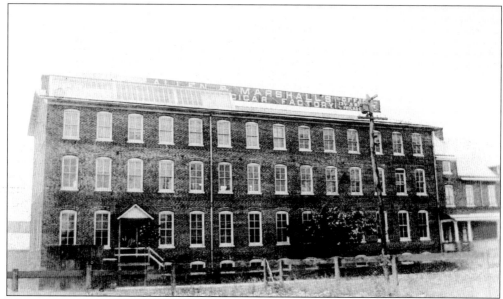

The Allen and Marshall Cigar Company occupied this large brick building at 218 New Street, which in 1935 was adapted to manufacture fur coats. Furriers came to town and hired Ray M. Taylor, who had experience in silk mills, as supervisor. He later acquired the business and became the largest manufacturer of fur coats in Pennsylvania. Known for their fine quality, the coats were sold in fine department stores in the nation's large cities. In 1938, he began retailing his coats at this factory.

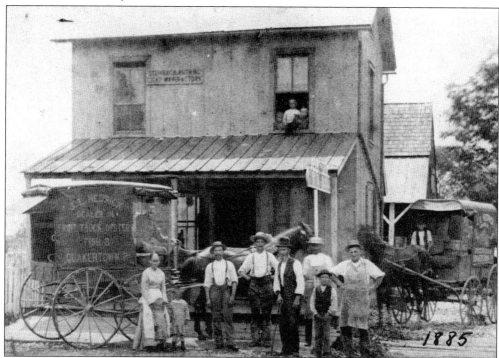

In 1885, Henry Ruth took this picture of a building on North Hellertown Avenue. Ruth owned a cigar factory on the second floor, and John Hetrick owned a grocery store on the first floor.

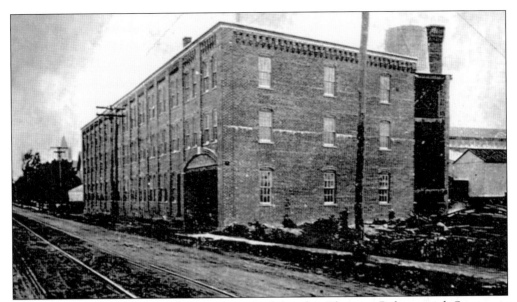

The Quakertown Stove Works was originated by the Thomas, Roberts and Stevenson Company in 1866 and gradually grew until it was destroyed by fire in 1881. A new firm, Rodgers, Scypes and Company, replaced the works in 1882. Stoves, heaters, and ranges were produced in this building on West Broad Street, between Third and Fourth Streets. Today, collectors highly value these stoves, which are occasionally discovered in older dwellings or in antiques shops. The Quakertown Stove Works building was demolished on November 30, 1966, to make room for the downtown shopping center and parking lot.

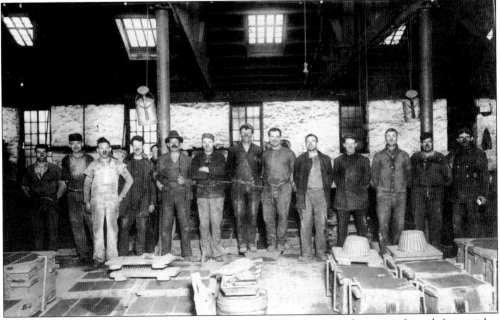

Posing inside the Quakertown Stove Works in 1918, these workers are, from left to right, Edward Henry, Elmer Auer, Ellwood Haines, Oscar Foulke, Elmer Jordan, William Kuschel, William Eckert, William Yost, Harvey Groff, William Fluck, Herbert Foulke, Jacob Weikel, Joseph Wismer, and George Cassel.

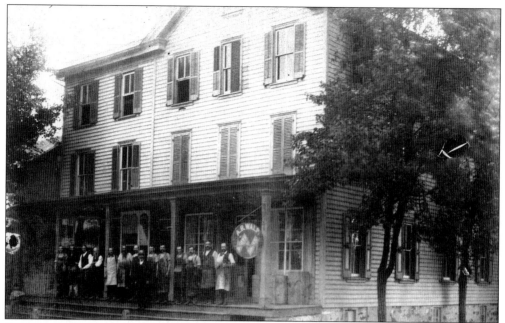

For three generations, this building at 122 East Broad Street was the home of a boot and shoe manufacturing business. In 1857, Aaron B. Walp joined his father, Charles Walp, in the business. In 1886, Aaron's son Tilghman took over operation of the factory. It was also in this building that Walp's employees started the Quakertown Band. Aaron was the great-great-grandfather of Nancy Walp Bosworth, historian of the Quakertown Historical Society. The building later became the Quakertown Furniture Store.

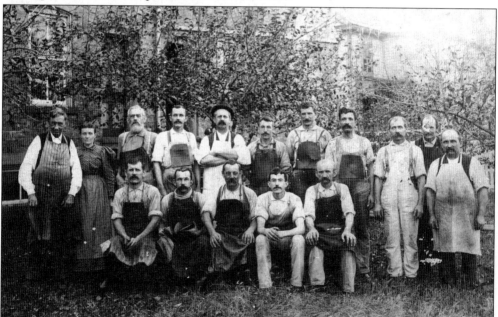

Mustaches seemed to be popular with the male workers at Scheida Shoe Factory, on the corner of South Hellertown Avenue and Franklin Street. Originally a cigar box factory, the building was later converted into apartments.

Harvey Stoneback is standing in his office in his early planing mill on Park Avenue near Front Street, later the site occupied by J.G. Furniture. Today, part of the building is used by Theatre Solutions, a company that gained attention in 2002 when it supplied 3,600 custom auditorium chairs with illuminated glass end panels for the Kodak Theatre in Los Angeles, the new home of the annual Academy Awards presentations.

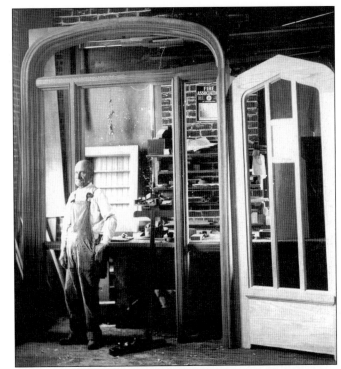

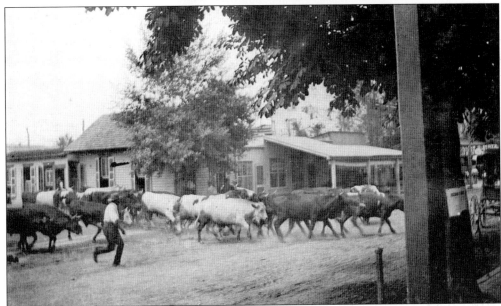

After being unloaded from railway freight cars, these cattle are being driven around Hager Brothers Meat Market at Second Street and West Broad Street. They are probably headed to the Fourth Street barn of Fred P. Fisher, president of the Canadian and Wisconsin Dairy Cow Company, who imported and sold cattle throughout eastern United States. The sign for the Canadian and Wisconsin Dairy Cow Company hangs over the inside door at the Quakertown Historical Society Market Place. Established by William Hager in 1897, the Hager family conducted the meat market for half a century.

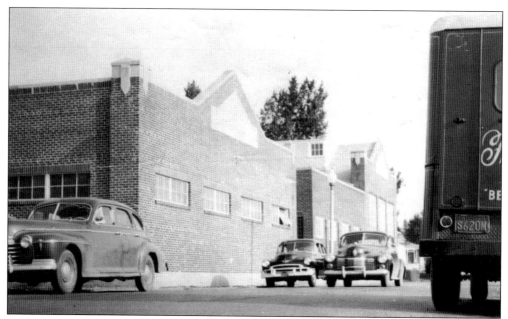

In the years prior to World War II and the invention of nylon, the knitting of full-fashioned silk hosiery was an important local industry. John S. Fisher owned the Best Made Hosiery Company housed in this building on Fifth Street, now occupied by Spinlon Industries. True to its name, Best Made Hosiery was widely marketed.

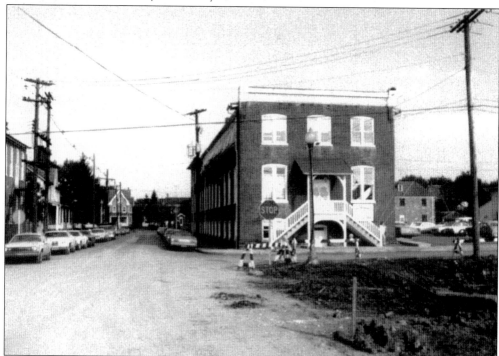

Many local men, and especially women, found employment as seamstresses in this brick building at the corner of Belmont and Erie Avenues. Here, John L. Renninger owned and operated the John L. Renninger Men's Trousers Manufacturing Company from 1929 to 1970.

Five

TAKING CARE
OF BUSINESS

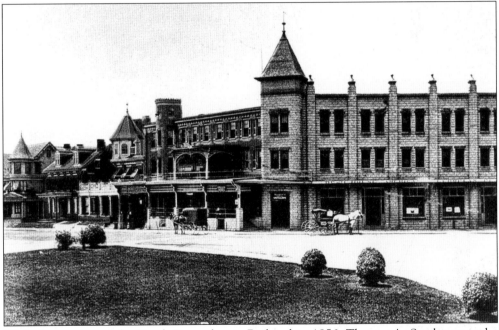

With the coming of the North Pennsylvania Railroad in 1856, Thomas A. Snyder erected a building on Front Street across from the railroad station. Its three stories and upper gallery were gracefully proportioned. This original part of the building is to the left of the high stone tower. It was referred to as the Quakertown Station Hotel. In 1863, William H. Bush bought the building and operated the hotel, finally changing its name in 1874 to the Bush House Hotel, the name it carries today. In 1882, Bush decided to retire and advertised the sale of his hotel. Included with the property was a cattle yard with stables for 25 cows, 100 hogs, 50 horses, and 6 building lots. In 1884, Henry H. Souder acquired the hotel and enlarged it. He added the stone observation tower and elaborately redecorated the interior. By 1905, it was regarded as the most commodious hotel between Philadelphia and Allentown. Souder's granddaughter Muriel Souder Hill and her husband, Russell Hill, managed it for some time before their son-in-law William Rissmiller assumed the role. He sold the 63-room hotel to its present owners, Paul and Yvonne Rhoades, in 1983.

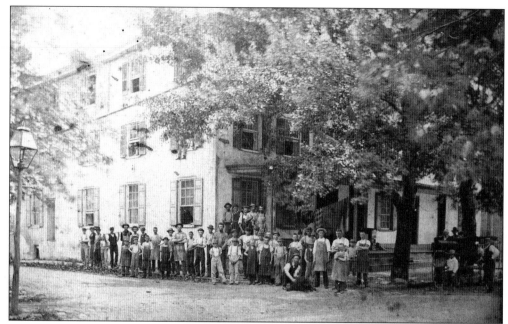

Built *c.* 1747 at the intersection of two American Indian trails, the Red Lion Inn provided food and lodging for travelers on the Philadelphia-to-Bethlehem turnpike. Originally called McCool's Inn, the structure at Main and West Broad Streets had two stories with a fireplace in every room. Nearby was a stable that had a guest register for registering horses. The people in front of the hotel may have been workers at the nearby James Harley Harness Company.

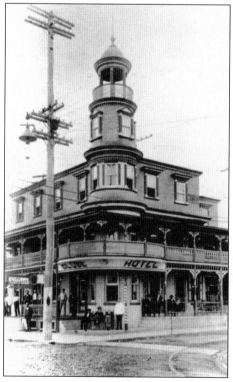

Originally a two-story house with a garret built *c.* 1827 by John Strawn, a potter, the Globe Hotel at East Broad Street and Belmont Avenue underwent several additions in 1875 and 1892, resulting in its Victorian appearance seen here. With the arrival of the railroad in 1856, the hotel's significance grew. The coming of the railroad made Quakertown increasingly important as a business and cultural center. The hotel now contains residential apartments.

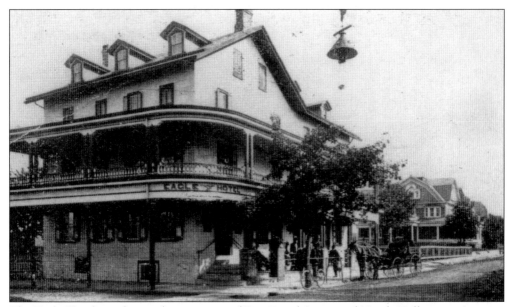

The Eagle Hotel, on the northeast corner of East Broad Street and North Hellertown Avenue, was in existence as early as 1832. Until it was annexed into the borough of Quakertown in 1874, downtown was known as Richland Centre. Records indicate the existence of a tavern on this corner and a store on the opposite corner as early as 1782. Former proprietors of the Eagle Hotel include Edwin Scheetz (1856), Francis and Joseph Hartman, Henry Ahlum, and Norman Kenderdine (1950). The hotel is currently undergoing renovations.

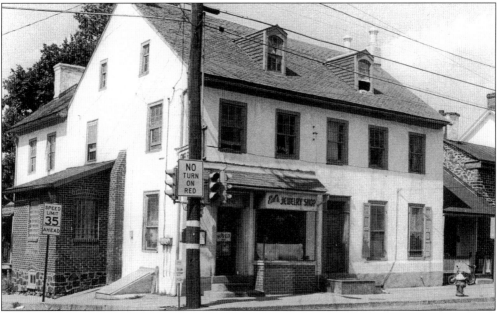

At 1239 West Broad Street on the northeast corner of the intersection with Main Street stands the first brick house built in town. William Green constructed the house in 1805 for use as a grocery store and post office. For many years, the room over the kitchen housed the book collection of the Richland Library Company. Liberty Hall, on the extreme right, is no longer connected to this building.

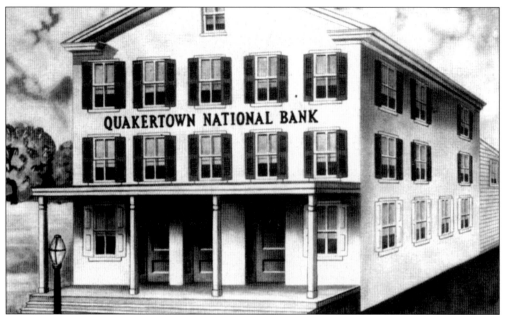

Securing its charter as a national bank in 1877, the Quakertown National Bank opened in this building at 312 West Broad Street, built by the Sons of Herman and later occupied by the *Free Press*. The bank's first president was Dr. Joseph G. Thomas. It was the only bank in Bucks County north of Doylestown. In 1903, the bank moved to a large building on the southeast corner of Third and West Broad Streets. In 1973, the bank moved to its present location, the colonial-styled building at the northeast corner of Third and West Broad Streets.

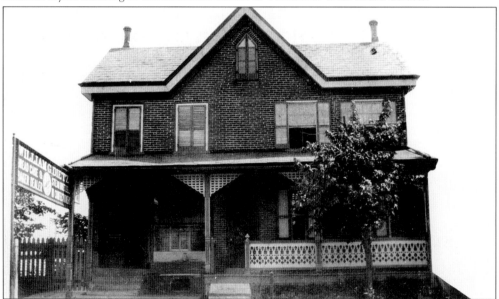

German-born William G. Dietz and his wife, Philopena, settled in town in 1876 and opened this bakery on West Broad Street where Sine's now stands. The bakery became famous for being the best one between Philadelphia and Allentown. By offering quality baked goods, the store released homemakers from the endless chore of baking bread. Dietz was one of the organizers of Bethel United Evangelical Church, later the United Methodist Church.

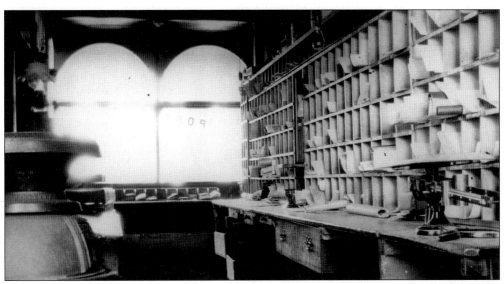

In earlier years, the post office was located in the home of private citizens and was rather frequently relocated. This is thought to be the post office in 1886, located at 132 South Main Street. It has a glass storefront, indicating that the premises may also have offered groceries for sale.

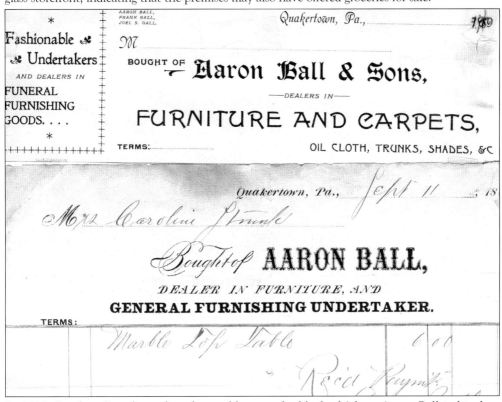

In 1880, Caroline Strunk purchased a marble-topped table for $6 from Aaron Ball in his shop on East Broad Street. Ball was an undertaker and a cabinetmaker. This special pairing of occupations was common in earlier times, for people went to furniture makers to have caskets made.

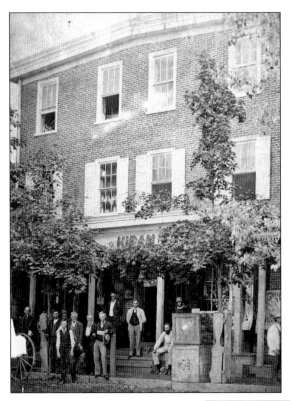

It is believed that this view of the Hiram Tice dry goods and variety store on West Broad Street in the Weidner building predates 1888. Records show that Francis C. Deaterly bought the store from Tice in 1906 and conducted a dry goods business until 1945, when his son Paul bought the store and continued the business until the 1960s.

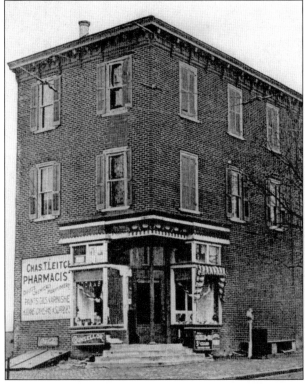

Pharmacist Charles T. Leitch owned and operated this drugstore at the southeast corner of West Broad Street and Main Street. It was the oldest drugstore in Upper Bucks, having been founded by Evan Penrose more than 75 years earlier. (Russell Leitch, the young son of Charles T. Leitch, died in France two days after the Armistice was signed.)

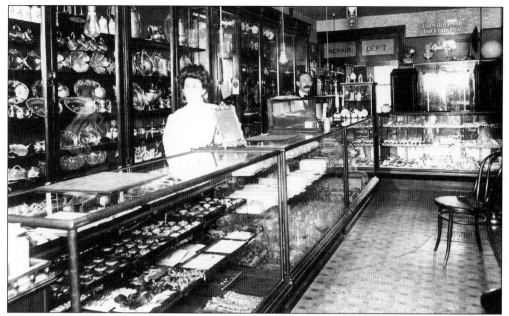

Originally located in the Goldsmith family home on Tenth Street, Goldsmith's Jewelry Store was moved to this location at 242 West Broad Street next to the Quakertown National Bank in 1886. In this 1906 picture of the store's interior, one can see pocket watches and cameo brooches in the display counter in the foreground, and crystal and silver serving pieces on the enclosed shelves. Gladys Goldsmith Allison was the third generation to operate the store.

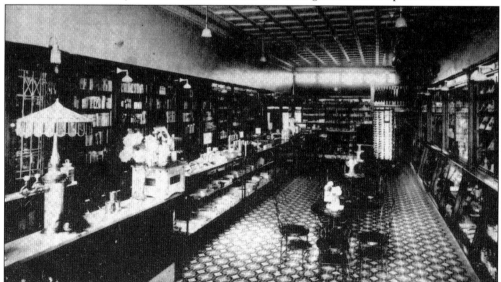

Moyer's drugstore on West Broad Street, pictured here c. 1912, was fitted with well-crafted cabinets, which have been preserved by Edward Cohen, longtime owner and operator of the Quakertown Drug Store. Moyer sold the store to Leroy Hillegass, pharmacist, from whom Cohen's father purchased it. Cohen is justifiably proud of its original furnishings, including beveled glass showcases and a custom-made drug cabinet that was transported by horse and wagon from Philadelphia. Moyer's total bill for the cases, their delivery, their three-day installation, and food for the workmen totaled a mere $40.

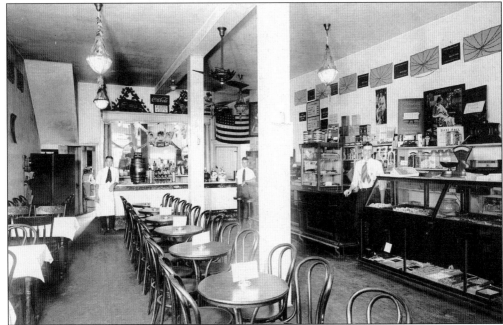

Allen Rothrock owned this restaurant on West Broad Street at the site that later became the New York Department store. Rothrock, on the right, and assistant Norman Frank, on the left, served ice cream, sodas, and candy. (The young man in the center is unidentified.) This picture was taken *c.* 1922.

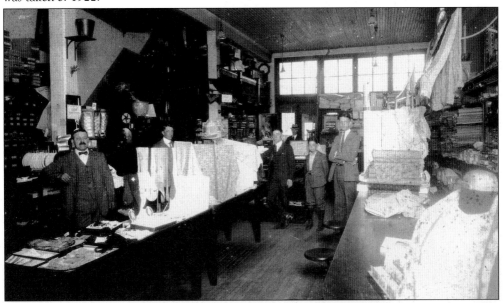

Oswin Gussman and his partner, Claude T. Rufe, operated a dry goods store in the Moyer building at 215 West Broad Street until their retirement in 1923, when Charles Ort and Asher Biehn assumed control. The store offered something for everyone. On the first floor, pictured, was menswear, on the left, and dry goods and notions, on the right. Upstairs, the store featured women's clothing and children's toys. Posing for the camera are, from left to right, Joseph Auchy, Charles Ort, Asher Biehn, Frederick Ort, and James Ort.

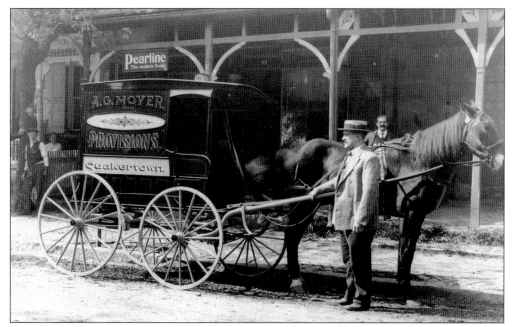

Carson Weber is standing in front of the delivery wagon for Moyer's store at 30 South Main Street between the Richland Library and the Red Lion Inn. The man in the background is unidentified. Prior to being operated by the Moyers, it was known as Artman's store. Following the Moyers, around 1932, it was operated by William Kaufman, who dealt in merchandise, and later by Frank and May Schumann, who sold groceries.

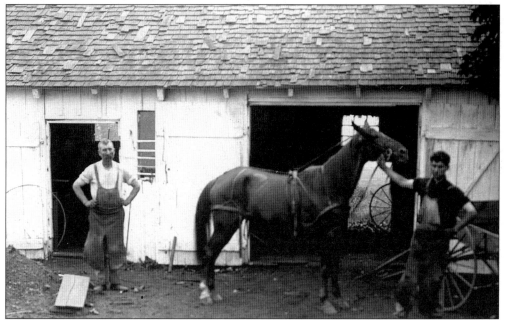

S.J. Reider, blacksmith and wheelwright, stands at his shop on Front Street in 1932. His son S.J. Reider Jr. is holding the horse they had fitted with new shoes. In a news account for that year, Reider said that only a few horses were kept in town. He estimated that about 300 were kept near town. There were only two other blacksmiths left in town—Harry Groman and Ervin Loux.

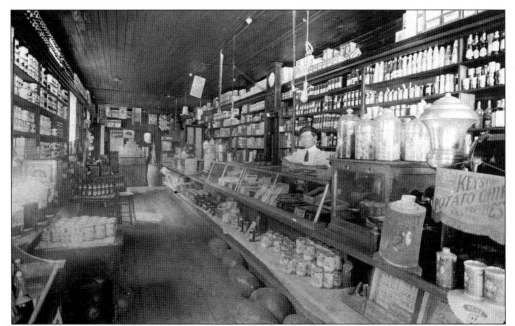

William Clemmer, salesclerk, awaits customers at A.E. Flagler's grocery store, at the southwest corner of Third and West Broad Streets. This picture was probably taken in the very early 1900s. In 1932, a new Woolworth building was erected on this site. That building is now occupied by the Friendly Book Store.

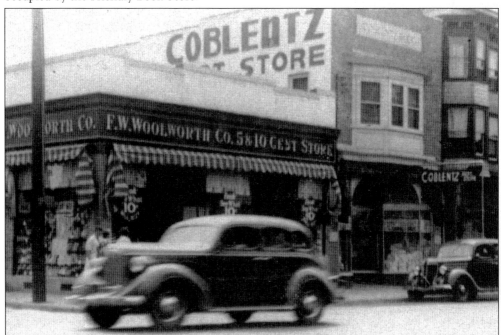

The F.W. Woolworth store, on the southwest corner of Third and West Broad Streets, cost $30,000 to build in 1932. Next door, Abraham Coblentz founded Coblentz Department Store, which sold clothing for the entire family. Men could buy wool two-pants suits for $12.50, and women could buy two silk dresses for $5.00.

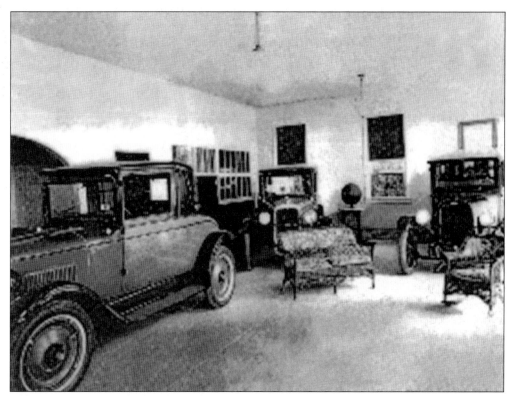

Alfred Johnson and Hobart Biehn, brothers-in-law, owned and operated the Johnson and Biehn Chevrolet Agency at 211 East Broad Street for 50 years. The showroom is pictured in 1929.

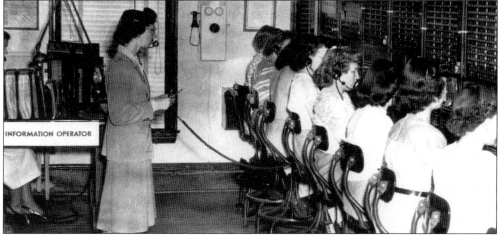

In 1947, the Bell Telephone Company office was located in the Merchants National Bank building, at West Broad and Second Streets. Pictured in that office are Bell employees, from left to right, Kathryn Fosbenner Krikory, information operator; Grace Leister Charles, supervisor; and switchboard operators Lois Snyder, Sara Detweiler, Helen Pancygrau, Betty Lucky Newhard, Mary Ewaniuk Pancygrau, Marie Polk Kuhn, Helen Hallman Eager, and Hazel Smoll Slotter.

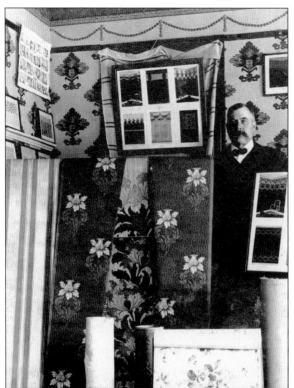

Frank H. Fluck, council member and paperhanger, sold wallpaper at 1408 West Broad Street and later turned the business over to his son Ralston B. Fluck. Frank Fluck's daughter Eunice built the Green Lantern Tea Room, which later became the Colonial Convalescent Home. Today, the La Piazza Café and several small shops occupy the site.

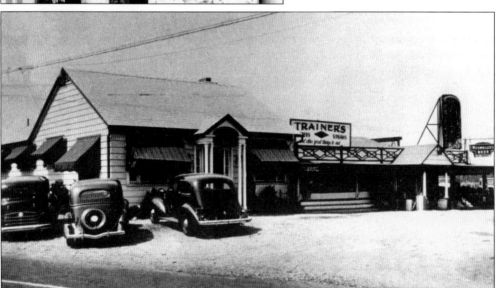

Mr. and Mrs. Ray Trainer founded Trainer's Restaurant on Route 309 in January 1932, during the Great Depression. They began with a small produce stand, a small counter, four booths, and tables. Trainer's reputation for fine food grew rapidly, and by 1969, its expanded dining room seated 850. Destroyed by fire when workmen were removing paint on July 4, 1975, the restaurant was rebuilt. Unfortunately, its halcyon days were over, and it was bought by Seafood Shanty. On July 11, 1995, it was torn down and replaced by a McDonald's, which is part of the shopping complex named Trainer's Corner.

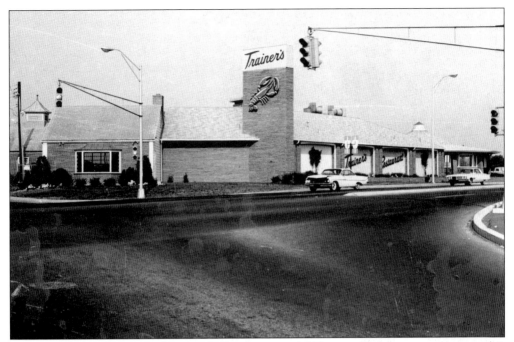

This is probably the view of Trainer's Restaurant indelibly inscribed in most townspeople's minds because the building features the familiar lobster signs. One lobster sign is now on the rear wall of TGI Fridays, located slightly north of the former Trainer's location.

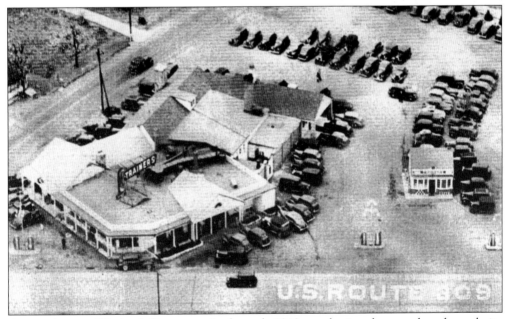

An aerial view of Trainer's Restaurant in the early 1940s emphasizes the growth and popularity of this well-known dining place. A service station can be seen to the right, facing Route 309, which is shown in the bottom of the picture.

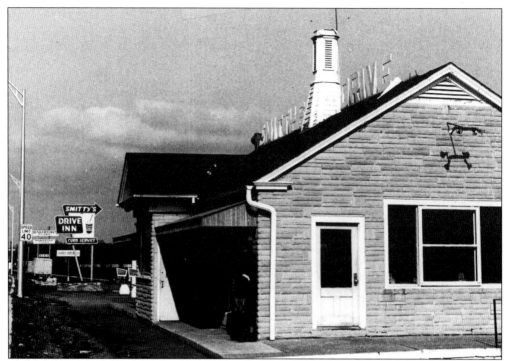

Smitty's, located on Route 309 across from Trainer's, was the swinging teenage hangout of the 1950s. The owner, Smitty, was noted for his creation of the Weber, a cheese steak to which he added lettuce, tomato, and mayo. The building has now become the Quakertown Family Restaurant.

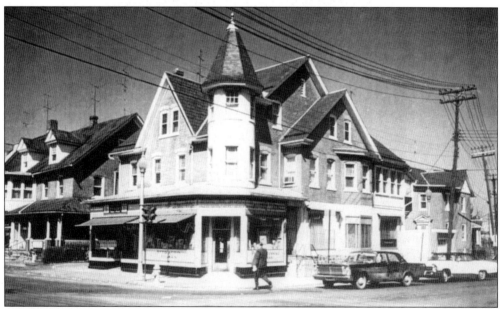

A.F. Muehlhauser erected this building containing a cigar store and residence at Third and West Broad Streets. The building was later owned by his son William W. Muehlhauser. It was razed in 1968 to make way for the downtown redevelopment project, which added the Quaker Village Shopping Center and triangle parking lot and which changed the roadway plan.

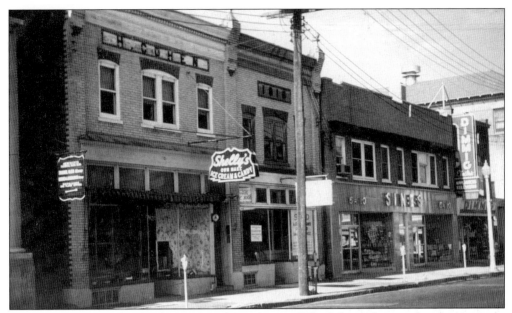

This view of the south side of West Broad Street east of Third Street features four businesses in the early 1960s—Shelly's (an ice cream and candy store), the vacated Friendly Book Store, Sine's, and Dimmig Electric. Sine's is the only store remaining in this location. Sine's opened in 1912 and is still operated by the founding family. It features an old-fashioned, popular lunch counter and is noted for its memorabilia of vintage Quakertown.

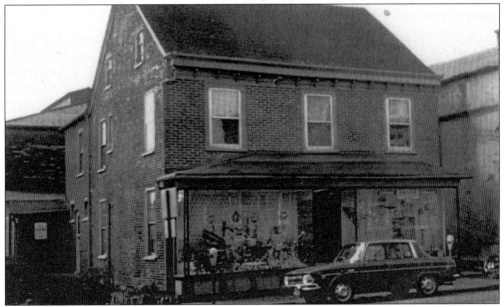

Klein's House Furnishings Store, at 116 East Broad Street, was opened for business in 1904 by Adolph and Mamie Klein. Their daughter Ethel Klein Lippman operated the store until the early 1990s. They kept a well-stocked and well-run business, offering everything a general merchandise store typically would offer. Customers enjoyed the mix of old stock and contemporary items. Townspeople were fond of saying, "If you can't find it at Klein's, you can't find it anywhere."

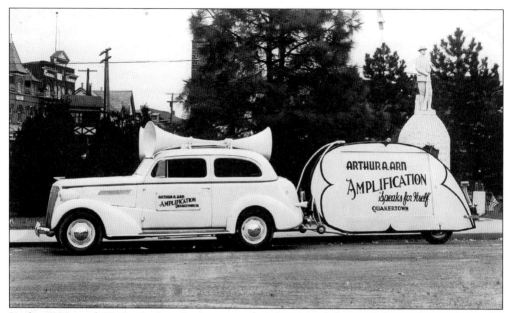

In the 1930s and 1940s, Arthur A. Arn owned and operated this mobile amplification system consisting of a car fitted with three loudspeakers on the roof. Paul V. Scheetz would announce special sales being held at local businesses, sporting events, carnivals, and special programs as he and Arn drove slowly up and down the streets of Quakertown. A trailer behind the car displayed advertisements.

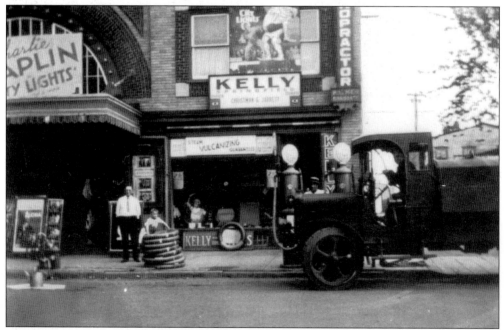

In addition to its theater auditorium, the Palace Theatre building housed the offices of a chiropractor on the second floor and a service station on the first floor. Notice the early bubble-headed gasoline pumps and the pile of inner tubes needed for the Kelly tires being sold. The building now houses Dimmig Electric.

Six
SERVING OUR COUNTRY

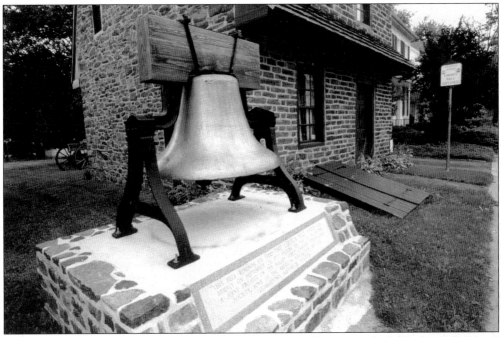

It is believed that on September 23, 1777, our nation's then uncracked Liberty Bell "slept" overnight under a pile of hay behind this small house at 1235 West Broad Street. After colonial forces were defeated by the British at the battle at Brandywine and at the Paoli Massacre, 200 troops evacuated the Bell, church bells, and other valuables from Philadelphia. It was feared that British troops would melt down all bells for use as ammunition. Then named the State House Bell, the bell was transported on one of 700 wagons headed north where the bell was given a safe hiding place in Zion Reformed Church, Allentown. Troops encamped to the rear of Liberty Hall and in the Red Lion Inn diagonally across from the house, on Main Street. Liberty Hall was built in 1772 as an addition to a log house, which has since been torn down. Maintained by the Quakertown Historical Society, the house is now a museum. In 1997, a replica of the Liberty Bell was erected in front of the building, a daily reminder of the determination of forebears and a powerful symbol for those who have sacrificed to preserve the freedom that the Liberty Bell represents.

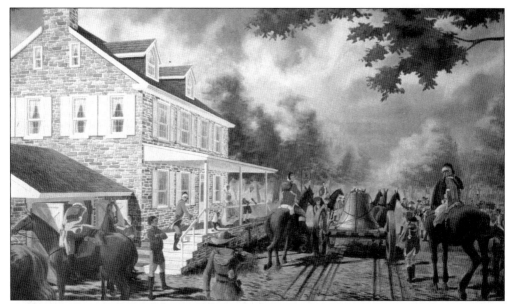

In this rendition of the Liberty Bell being transported over the stagecoach route from Philadelphia to Allentown, artist James Mann includes the Red Lion Inn (McCool's Tavern) as it would have looked in 1777. The livery stable is to the left. Troops are moving the bell north on Main Street and are headed for the rear grounds of a small house now known as Liberty Hall at 1235 West Broad Street.

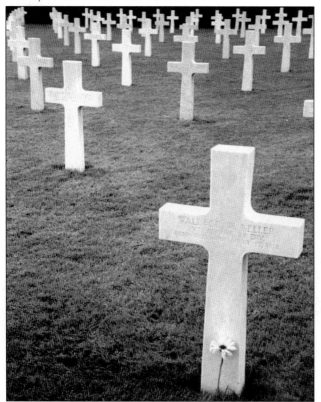

This simple cross in Belleau Wood in northern France marks the grave of Wallace Willard Keller of the 28th Division, the first Quakertown man killed in World War I. Here, U.S. Infantry and Marines were victorious over the enemy in the second battle of the Marne. In 1923, the site was dedicated as a memorial to American war dead. This photograph was taken by William Peischel in April 2001 on a visit to the site.

Seated is Wallace Willard Keller, for whom the Wallace Willard Keller Post 242, American Legion, was named in 1919. He died on July 18, 1918.

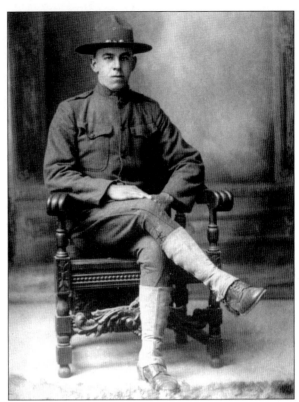

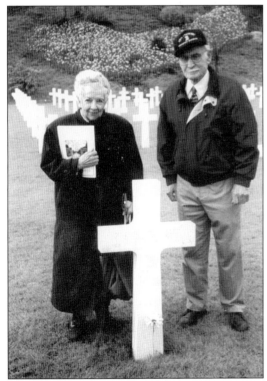

Janice and William Peischel are paying their respects to Wallace Willard Keller at his grave in Belleau Wood, France. The Peischels were visiting the site as part of a tour of battle sites by World War II survivors of the 26th Division. Peischel has been active in the Wallace Willard Keller Post for more than 50 years.

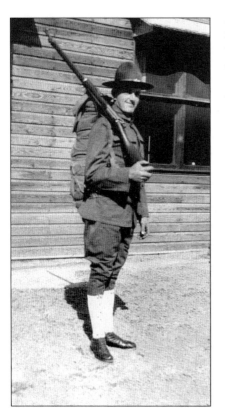

Russell Leitch was the young son of Charles T. Leitch, owner of the oldest drugstore in Upper Bucks County at 1232 West Broad Street. Russell Leitch served in World War I and died in France two days after the Declaration of Armistice in November 1918.

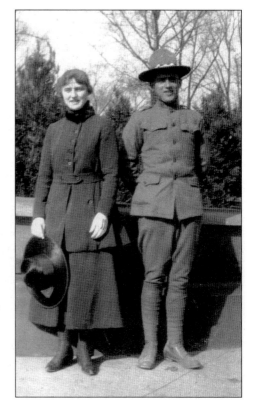

In his World War I uniform, Floyd H. Kilmer is seen courting Edna Biehn, whom he later married. After the war, Kilmer led in the formation of the Wallace Keller Post 242 of the American Legion and became its first commander. He served three terms as commander—in 1920, 1921, and 1922. Kilmer became a teacher and a guidance counselor at Quakertown High School. Edna also became a teacher at the high school.

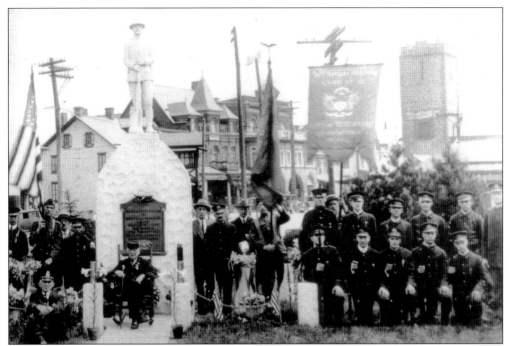

On May 30, 1926, this monument at Station Square was dedicated as a memorial to men who had served in the U.S. Army, Navy, and Marine Corps in World War I. Police Chief Harry Rhoades, seated in the lower left-hand corner, proposed the memorial and collected funds. Attending this ceremony were American Legion Post 242 members, Sons of the American Revolution (right), and the oldest survivor of the Civil War (seated in front of the monument). In 1966, the monument was moved to Memorial Park on Mill Street.

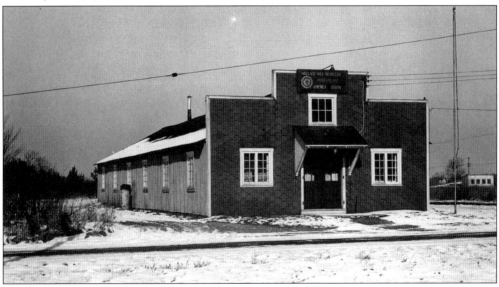

The former oyster shell mill on Mill Street was remodeled for use as a meeting quarters by the Wallace Willard Keller Post 242 of the American Legion in 1930. It provided a kitchen, meeting room, and storage. Prior meetings were held by the post in rented space in various buildings in town. The community swimming pool now occupies this area.

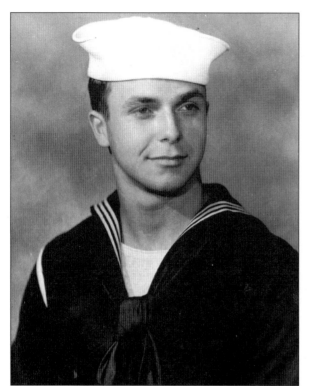

Alexander Biggs Keegan, 23, was one of 27 crewmembers who were lost when their U.S. Navy submarine, *Squalus*, sank off Portsmouth, New Hampshire, on May 23, 1939, during what was to be a routine training mission. Keegan was the eldest of Andrew and Mary Keegan's 10 children and a graduate of St. Isidore's School. At the Naval Board of Inquiry, it was revealed that Keegan had stayed at his post in order to warn companions that the battery room was filling up with water.

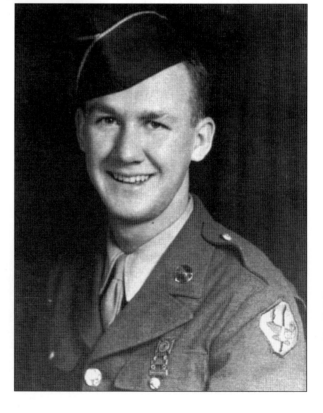

In a coma and suffering from a grave head wound, this soldier, without dog tags, was not identified in an English military hospital in 1945 until a chaplain noticed his Quakertown High School ring and discovered its inscription, "Weamer 1942." The chaplain wrote to the local chief of police, who contacted the *Free Press* editor, who then informed Weamer's parents. Interviewed recently, David Weamer said, "I don't remember a thing about two months of my life."

Orphaned at age seven, Johnny Rivers was taken in by the Elvin Horne family of Quakertown R.D. when he was 13. He graduated from Quakertown High School, where he was known for his athletic prowess and built a reputation in the area as a boxer. He later enlisted in the U.S. Marines. Rivers and two of his buddies are credited with gunning down 200 of the enemy before he was mortally wounded on August 21, 1942, on Guadalcanal. Pres. Franklin D. Roosevelt cited Rivers for bravery and awarded him the Navy Cross posthumously.

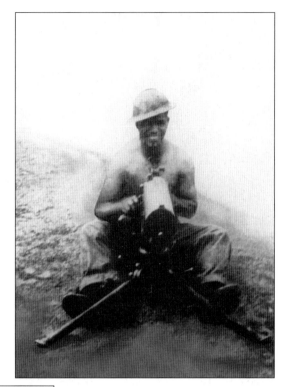

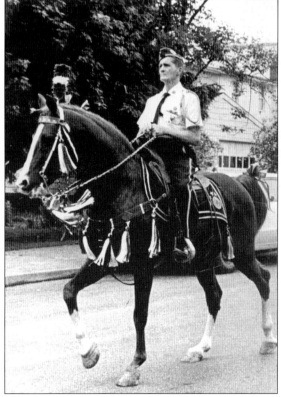

Quakertown's many parades have been highlighted by John Keithan, who is leading the parade riding his horse, Reds. Keithan, a baker by trade, is also a veteran of World War II.

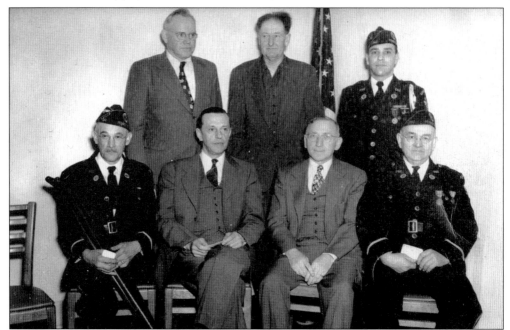

In July 1950, the Wallace Willard Keller Post 242, American Legion, dedicated its new building at Park Avenue and Fourteenth Street. Honored at this ceremony were veterans of World War I. Seated, from left to right, are Roland Frederick, Bert Knerr, Sol Schacter, and Clint Krout. Standing are Robert Eichner, on the left, and Zeno Campbell, in the center. Standing on the extreme right is the post commander in 1950, William Becker, a World War II veteran.

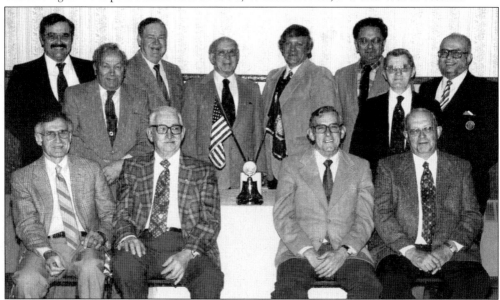

Honored at the Commanders' Ball for serving as commanders of American Legion Post 242 are, from left to right, the following: (front row) William Peischel (1956), Leroy Mease (1962), William Edge (1953), and Henry Landis (1952); (back row) Joseph Glazier (1981, 1997), Leon Lewis (1959), Charles Stewart (1968), Morris Todd (1960), Kenneth Williams (1983–1991, 1996), George Banas (1969), John Keithan (1975, 1980), and Russell Schanely (1964).

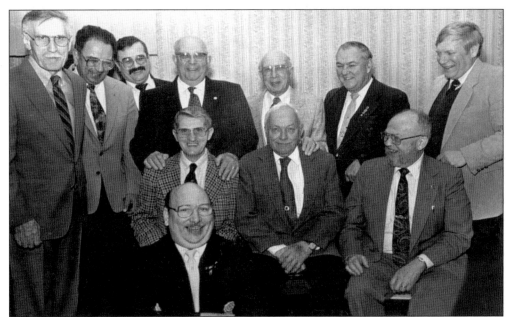

A laughing group of veterans who served as commanders of American Legion Post 242 is assembled at this reunion ceremony. Seated in the front row is Charles L. Wahl. Seated in the middle row from left to right are John H. Keithan (1975, 1980), Leon W. Lewis (1959), and Russell Schanely (1964). Standing from left to right are William Peischel (1956), George Banas (1969), Joseph V. Glazier (1981, 1997), Henry W. Landis (1959), Morris B. Todd, (1960), Alfred G. Shannon (1979), and Kenneth Williams (1983–1991 and 1996).

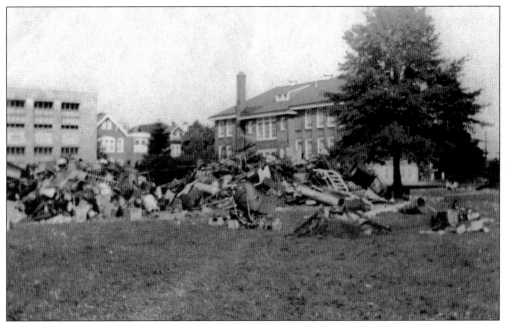

This is the way the playing fields adjacent to Quakertown High School and the Lincoln School looked in September 1942. Students had collected 75 tons of scrap metal to be recycled for the war effort. The fields are adjacent to Park Avenue, between Sixth and Seventh Streets.

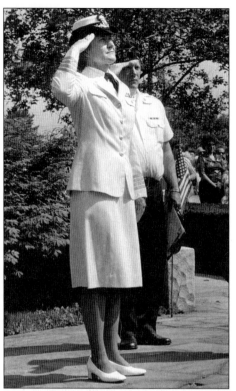

Navy Capt. Jane Renninger, now retired, is shown saluting the flag at Memorial Day services in 1985, when she was the guest speaker. An alumnus of Quakertown Community Senior High School, Class of 1961, Renninger was commissioned in 1965. She served as commanding officer of four navy commands, two of them major commands with more than 1,200 personnel. During her 27 years of service, she held technical and leadership positions that emphasized computer systems development and management.

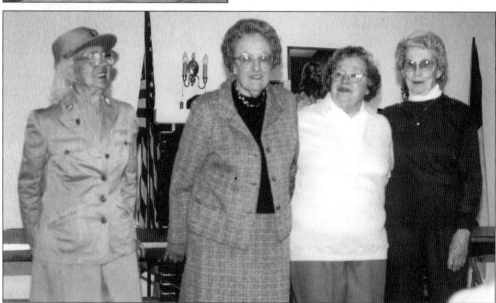

Quakertown Chapter 3377 of the American Association of Retired Persons honored three members who served in the armed forces in World War II. Evelyn Armstrong, on the left, is pictured in her Women's Army Corps uniform. Ann Cundiff, third from the left, was a second lieutenant in the Army Nurse Corps and in charge of psychiatric units. Gladys Trumbauer, on the far right, was a private in the Army Medical Corps. The coordinator of the program to commemorate Women's History Month in 1996, Carolyn Potser, is second from the left.

Seven

SERVING OUR COMMUNITY

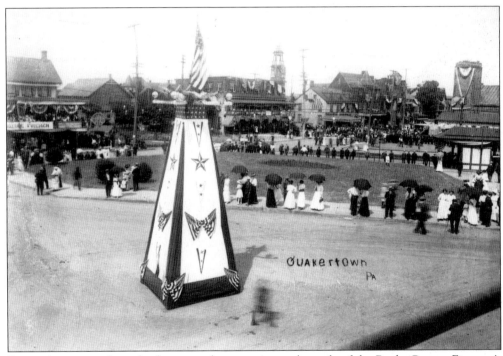

Pictured is a scene from the first annual convention and parade of the Bucks County Firemen's Association held in town in June 1914. The parade is marching from East Broad Street to West Broad Street, about to cross the railroad tracks. The parade was the first of many firemen's parades hosted by local fire companies. Even before firehouses were constructed, firefighters arranged for hose carriages to be stored in various buildings. Fire Company No. 1, organized in 1882, first occupied quarters in the wooden borough hall on West Broad Street until 1907, when it built a brick firehouse on Fourth Street. In 1920, it left this building and returned to the borough hall. In 1938, a new borough hall and firehouse was constructed at the West Broad Street location. In 1925, a segment of Fire Company No. 1 separated to form West End Fire Company No. 2, and moved to Main Street. In 1957, this company moved to its present quarters on Park Avenue. In 1972, Fire Company No. 1 moved to its new firehouse at Fifth and West Broad Streets. Today, both volunteer companies and their auxiliaries work steadfastly at fundraising and at protecting the public.

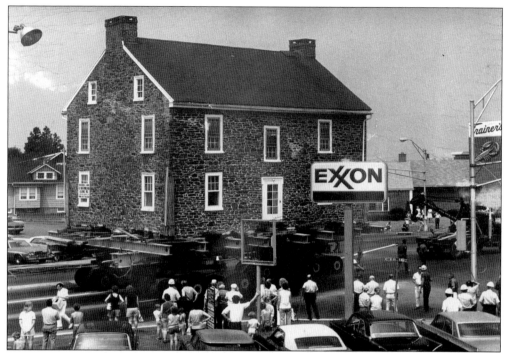

Excitement was in the air that summer day in 1974 when this stone house, built in 1812 by Quaker Edward Foulke, was moved from its original setting in the southwest part of town on Trumbauersville Road to its present home on North Main Street. When developers planned to raze the building to make way for the Country Square Shopping Center, the Quakertown Historical Society developed a daring plan to save the building: borrow $40,000 to finance the relocation and pay off the loans with fundraisers. The picture below shows the building with its lattice side porch as it appeared in 1974 just before it was moved.

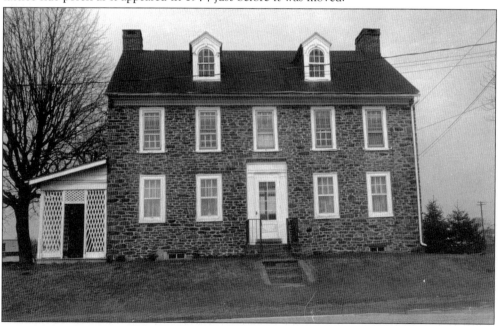

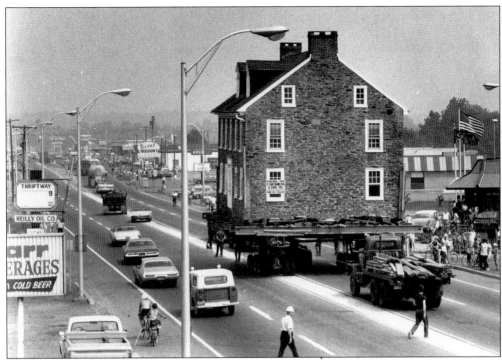

The pictures at the top left and top right record the community effort to move the building north on Route 309 to reach its present home. The Quakertown Historical Society named the house the Burgess Foulke House after Edward Foulke's son who was the first burgess (mayor) of Quakertown. The contemporary view below is one of the gifts the society has given to the town. The society uses the house and the Market Place Barn across the street as museums to display artifacts, including bequests that help perpetuate local history. Seen visiting the house are descendants of Edward and Eleanor Foulke, who arrived in Philadelphia in 1698, according to Margaret Ann Foulke Hellman, family genealogist.

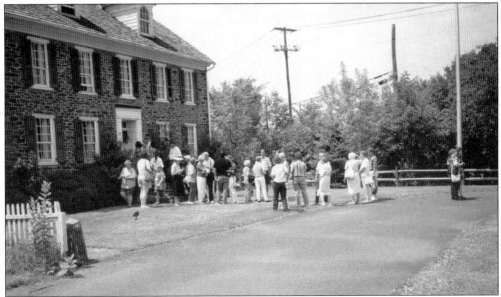

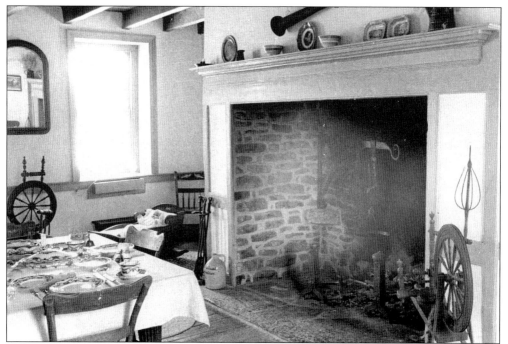

In this kitchen in the Burgess Foulke house, the walk-in fireplace has two warming shelves. Over the mantel is a long horn used by the stagecoach driver to announce arrivals and departures. Constructed with open beams and random-width floorboards, the room contains a flax spinning wheel, a 1700s cradle, and a plank table set with flow-blue china. Under the window is a drawer that disappears into the wall, probably used to pay farm hands directly through the window.

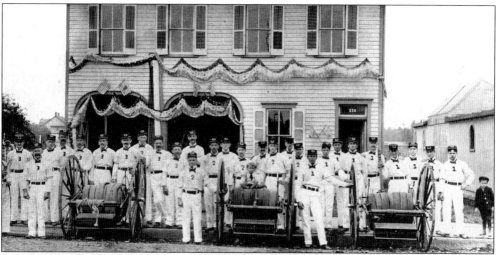

Quakertown Fire Company No. 1 was organized in 1882, chartered in 1886, and established its home in this building at 330 West Broad Street, which also housed the borough hall. The fire company was composed of three units, the First, Second, and Third Districts. William Kollo was the first chief. In 1938, this building was razed and a new structure built, which served as a borough hall and fire station until the present borough hall was built on North Third Street in 1974.

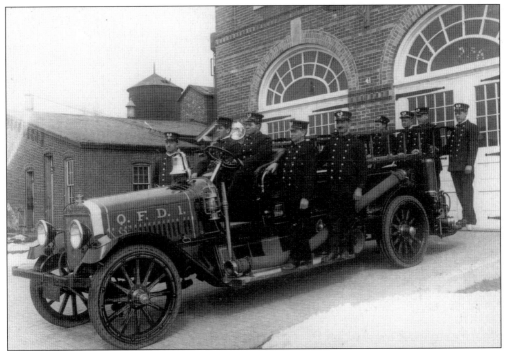

Members of Fire Company No. 1 are shown on their fire truck at their Fourth Street fire station, which was in use between 1907 and 1920. The original Quakertown Electric Light Plant building is to the left of the firehouse. Later, this location was occupied by the manufacturing companies of Endura, W.R. Grace, and FiberMark, respectively.

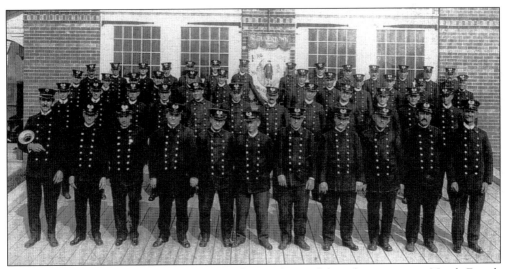

Firefighters of Fire Company No. 1 are standing in front of their fire station on North Fourth Street, sometime between 1907 and 1920. In 1920, they gave up this building and returned to the borough hall on West Broad Street. In 1938, a new firehouse and borough hall was constructed at the West Broad Street location.

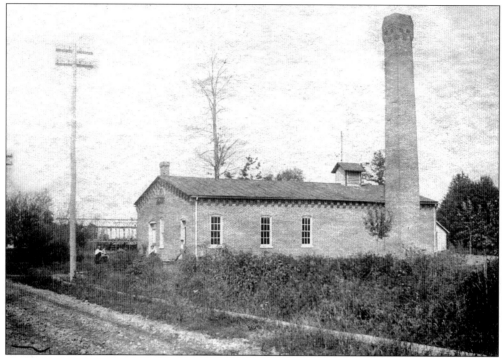

Quakertown's first electric light plant was built in 1896 on the east side of North Fourth Street next to Licking Run Creek on the site later occupied by manufacturing plants. When this picture was taken, the surrounding area was pasture land. Quakertown's burgess, J. Levi Heacock, was instrumental in overcoming difficulties in establishing the plant.

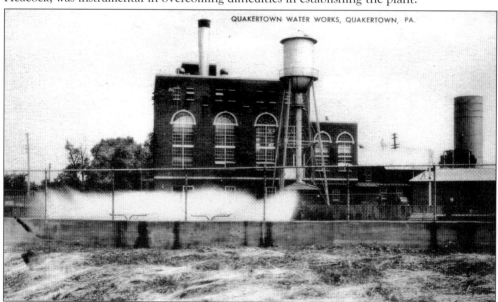

QUAKERTOWN WATER WORKS, QUAKERTOWN, PA.

Reconstructed in 1917 as the town's electric plant, this building on Erie Avenue was a municipally owned and operated plant that housed the new generator necessary for supplying light and power for all residences and industries. Never a burden on taxpayers, the plant produced profits that were used to build and operate a modern street-lighting system.

78

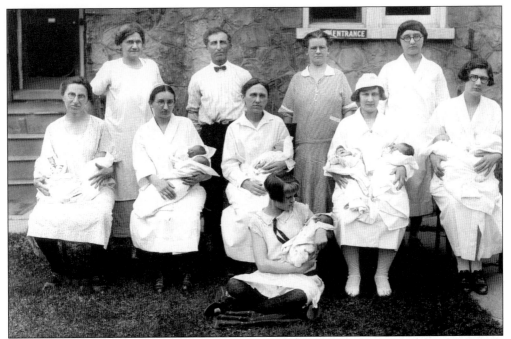

From 1921 to 1929, Emma G. Gehman operated Miss Gehman's Hospital and Convalescent Home at Third and Juniper Streets. One of its main functions was as a maternity hospital. Among the babies being held by these nurses on Gehman's staff are local residents Shirley Leister and Betty Wiead. The building became the Tice Clinic after the Quakertown Community Hospital was opened.

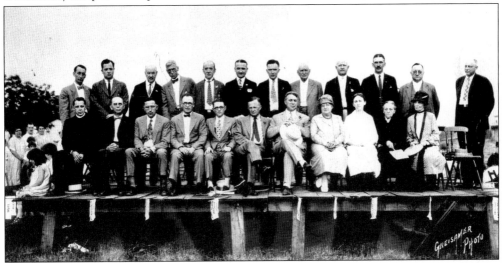

Community leaders recognized the need for a hospital and formed this committee for planning it in June 1927. From left to right are the following: (front row) Rev. H.W. Fitting, Rev. Jere Koehler, Joseph Cavanaugh, Rev. ? Marks, Asher Biehn, William Freed Sr., the unidentified campaign director, Mrs. Samuel Cressman, Emma Gehman, RN, Sally Thomas, and Mrs. Frank Ball; (back row) Lamar Hartman, William Muehlhauser, Jonas Harley, Dr. George Ozias, Samuel Cressman, Dr. Harvey Feigley, Dr. Raymond Tice, Reuben Freed, Erwin Ritter, Victor Smith, Dr. William Erdman, and Dr. Andrew Biehn.

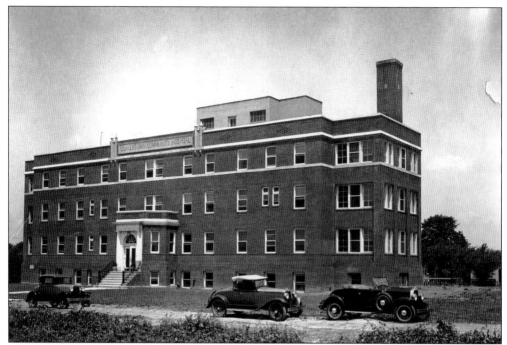

The Quakertown Community Hospital opened to care for patients in 1930. Notice that Park Avenue was not yet paved. Since then, several additions have been constructed. It is now St. Luke's Quakertown Hospital.

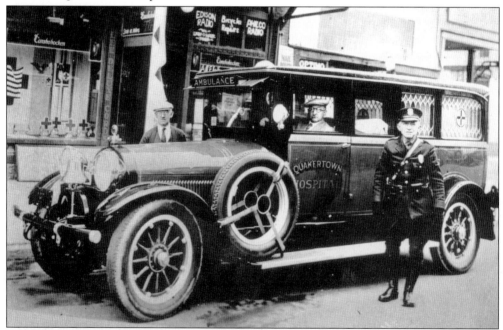

Frank Gehman built this first ambulance for use by the Quakertown Community Hospital. He is the driver seen here behind the wheel of the ambulance. Standing behind the vehicle is Irvin Hillegas. In front is Harry Rhoades, chief of police. This picture was probably taken in the early 1930s.

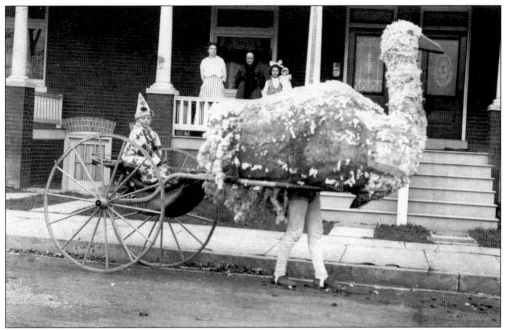

The people of Quakertown have always loved parades, including the Halloween parades, which are usually sponsored by service organizations. For the Halloween parade in 1916, Frank Hessler is wearing this ostrich costume. His six-year-old son, Harold, is in the driver's seat of the two-wheeled cart. Observing on the porch are Frank's wife, Matilda, on the left, and his daughter Florence, on the right, holding a doll. (The woman in the middle is unidentified.) We hope the Hesslers won a prize.

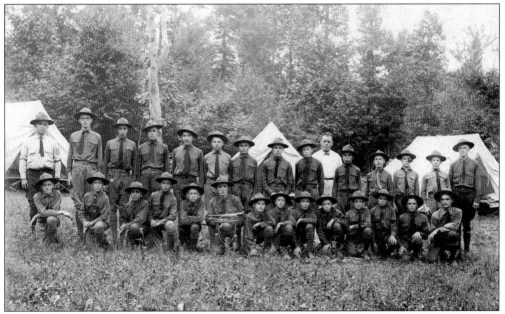

Quakertown Boy Scout Troop No. 1 is pictured in 1925 on a camping outing. Troop No. 1 was chartered in 1922 to the Wallace Willard Keller Post No. 242 of the American Legion. Troop No. 2 was organized in 1930, with O. Kenneth Fretz serving as scoutmaster.

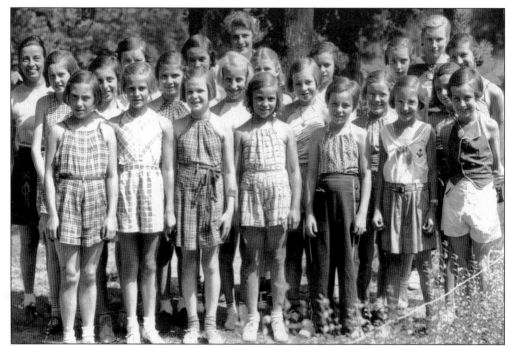

The broad smile on the face of Alverna Afflerbach, on the left in the back row, reveals her delight in being the leader of the town's first Girl Scout troop in 1936, called the Lone Star Troop I. Afflerbach remained active in scouting activities for 54 years. Several generations profited from her guidance and high ideals.

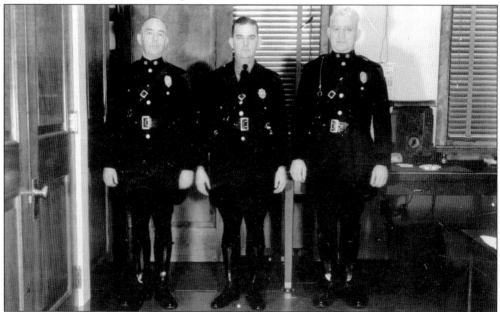

Standing at attention, ready to protect the public, are officers of the Quakertown Police Department in police headquarters in the former borough hall on West Broad Street. They are, from left to right, George Harr, chief of police Harry Welsh, and S.J. Reider Jr. This picture was probably taken in the late 1930s or early 1940s.

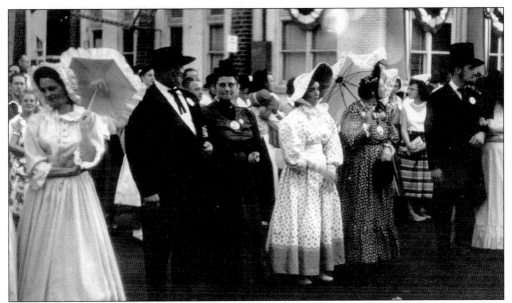

The year 1955 marked the 100th anniversary of the incorporation of Quakertown as a borough. A highlight of that year's celebration was, naturally, a parade. Townspeople entered into the spirit and dressed appropriately in period clothing. They called themselves the "brothers of the brush" and "sisters of the swish" as they adapted to beards or long skirts.

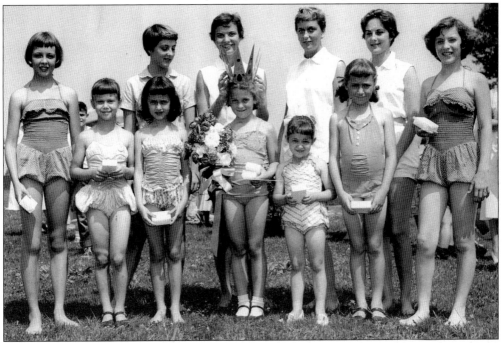

A junior centennial queen was selected in 1955 as part of the festivities for Quakertown's 100th anniversary celebration. She was Marcia Groff, wearing the crown and holding flowers. From left to right are the following: (front row) Sharon Hellman, Jeanie Burns, Tamson Moyer, Marcia Groff, Kathy George, Barbara Edge, and Margaret Moyer; (back row) Jane Lacey, Joyce Gerhart, Abby Viehe, and Judy Lacey.

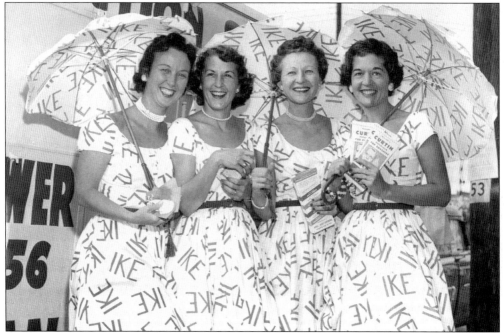

In 1956, the GOP bandwagon came to town and visited the headquarters of Citizens for Eisenhower in the Palace Theatre building. Four Republican women expressed their enthusiasm for Eisenhower by wearing dresses and carrying parasols imprinted with "IKE." The women are, from left to right, Kay Wisneski, Gladys Smoll, Mildred Rosenberger, and Dorothy Williams.

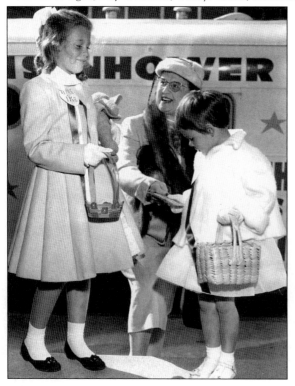

Margarette S. Kooker, elected to the General Assembly in 1955, was the first woman representative from Bucks County. She served under the leadership of Governors Leader, Lawrence, and Scranton before retiring in 1967. Here she is pictured in 1956 in front of the Eisenhower bandwagon with her granddaughter, on the left, Marcia Groff, daughter of Dr. and Mrs. Harvey Groff. (The girl on the right is not identified.)

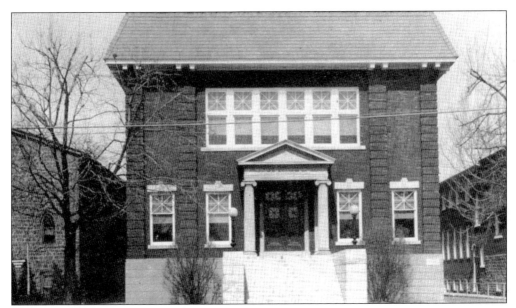

Dr. Joseph Thomas, an active Freemason, was one of the organizers of the Quakertown Masonic Lodge established in 1872. The Masons held their early meetings on the third floor of the Quakertown National Bank. The above building, at Fifth and West Broad Streets, has served as the Masonic Temple for many years.

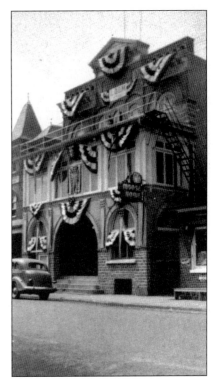

Quakertown Lodge No. 567, Loyal Order of the Moose, was founded in 1915 in the Hinkle building. The pictured building, at 113–115 East Broad Street, served as the lodge home for many years until its destruction by fire in 1976. In its reconstruction, four stories were reduced to two, and the building was back in operation in 1977. The Moose lends its wide financial support to social welfare.

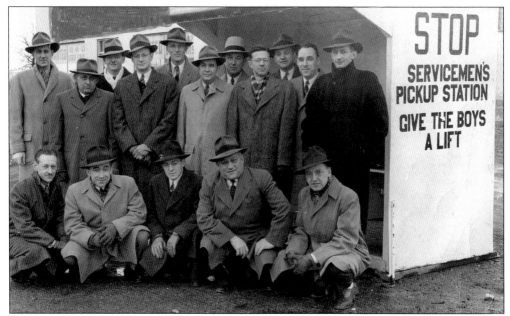

Posing in one of two shelters they erected in the early 1940s, these Lions Club members provided sheltered pick-up stations where servicemen could await a ride. From left to right are the following: (front row) Paul Dietz, Norman Stahl, Manny Klein, Harry Hoffman, and Ernest Bossert; (middle row) Russell Scheetz, an unidentified member, Frank Swartz, Clair Biehn, Jack Edge, and Gerald Rosengerger; (back row) Dean Zweier, Warren Diehl, Charles Whaland, and two unidentified members. Chartered in 1939, the Lions Club is still very active, placing emphasis, today, upon sight conservation projects.

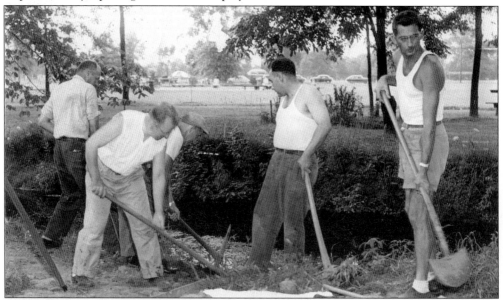

In 1952, members of the Quakertown Lions Club built a bridge over the creek to make Memorial Park accessible from the Broad Street entrance. At work in this picture are, from left to right, Charles Whaland, Skeetz Trumbauer, Jack Edge, and Gerald Rosenberger. The borough has since replaced this bridge.

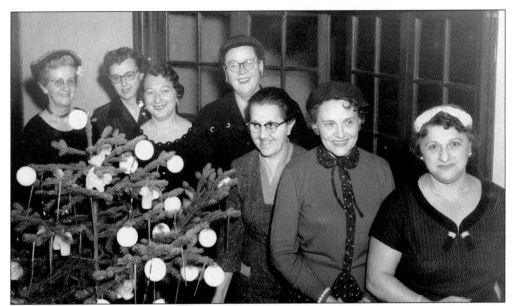

Although the Soroptimist Club no longer exists in town, for many years professional and business women enjoyed the camaraderie of membership activities. Since it was organized as a quota club, membership covered many types of work. Attending a 1950 Christmas party meeting in this picture are, from left to right, Mrs. A.N. Shea; Mary Shelly, W.R. Grace Company; Marian Mastin, Mastin's farms; Elizabeth Treffinger, Quakertown High School librarian; Miriam Steely, insurance agent; Maggie Sweinhart, Ice and Storage Company; and Esther Cohen, Quakertown Drug Store.

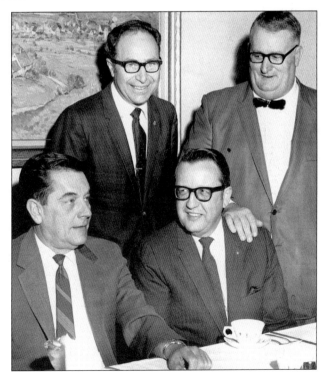

At a 1969 ceremony marking change in leadership, outgoing borough manager Guy Krapp (sitting to the left) yields to Nicholas Luca (standing to the left), new borough manager. Mayor Philip Richter is standing with his hand on the shoulder of Ernest Bossert, president of the borough council.

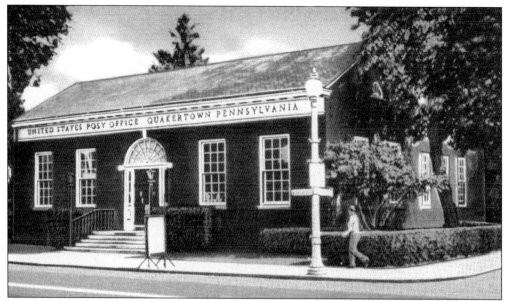

This brick building, at the corner of Fifth and West Broad Streets, served as Quakertown's post office from 1937 until its recent relocation to the California Road. Prior to 1937, the post office was housed in the Merchants National Bank building and in a store, both downtown. From its beginnings in 1803, however, the post office was located at various sites on or near Main Street for 111 years.

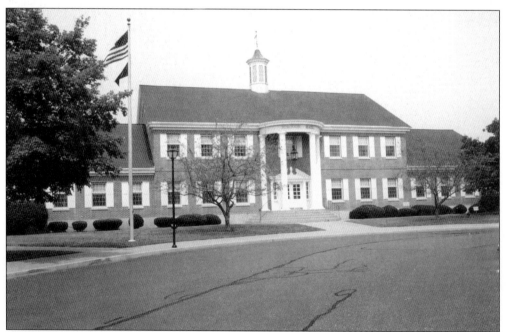

Our present borough hall, located off North Third Street, has served our community well since its dedication in 1975. It has provided needed space for borough offices and meetings, and for the police department. The hall replaces the one on West Broad Street, which was in use from 1938 to 1974.

Eight
PLAYING VARIOUS SPORTS

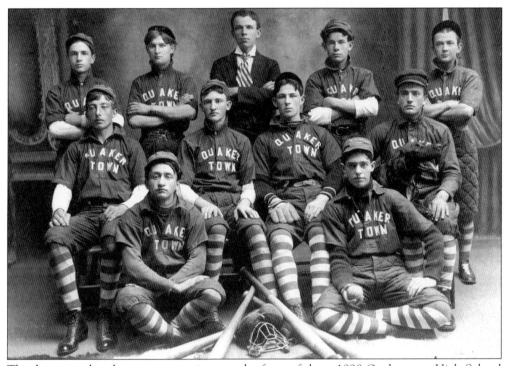

The determined and serious expressions on the faces of these 1898 Quakertown High School baseball players demonstrate the importance the Quakertown area has placed on sports since at least the late 1800s. As the area changed from a primarily agrarian culture to a more industrial and commercial one, people had more time to participate in sports and attend local athletic events. As the 20th century progressed, scholastic and community sports became more than mere pastimes. The area's ball fields and indoor facilities were places where young people developed strong character traits through intense competition and also provided opportunities for lifelong athletic participation. The Crescent Hill Tennis Club, Lulu Park's sulky and automobile races, American Legion baseball and basketball teams, Quakertown High School athletic teams, and the Quakertown Athletic Association are all part of this rich local sports tradition. A significant part of this history took place on the high school's Alumni Field and at the borough's Memorial Park. It was here that coaches such as Jake Stoneback, John O. Barth, and Marion Afflerbach—all local legends—inspired some of their players to become coaches and community leaders, perpetuating the positive aspects of local athletic competition.

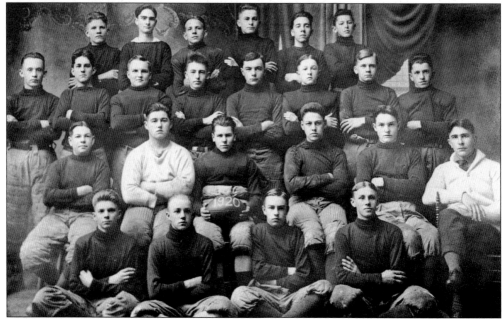

This 1920 Quakertown High School football team managed a fine 7-4 record under coach Jake Stoneback, despite an unsatisfactory high school athletic program. Stoneback and Earl A. Ball reorganized Quakertown High School athletics the following year, and the 1921 football team won the Bucks County championship. Lettermen on the 1920 team were Dewart Stover, Harold Stover, Charles Reinhart, Raymond Bortz, Wesley Dietz, Oswin Rufe, Reginald Beaford, Frederick Fisher, Stan Moyer, Elmer Lohman, Manasseh Hager, Joe Person, Morris Slifer, Lloyd Lobb, and Arthur Kelly.

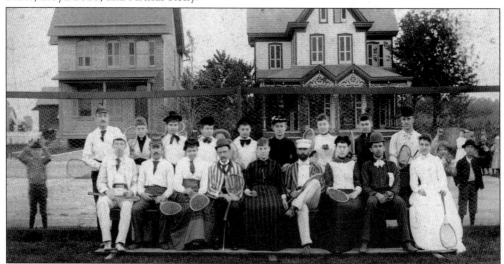

These dapper amateur athletes from 1883 honed their tennis skills at the Crescent Hill Tennis club, which was located in Quakertown Borough below Third and Juniper Streets. Included in the front row are Sam Berger, Fred Sommers, Mirnie Bush, Joe Ball, Anna Jordan, Ed Bush, Winnie Ozias, and Bob Sypes. Included in the back row are Herk Reinhard, Florence Moyer, Lillie Moyer, Carrie Ozias, Blanch Stoneback, Elmira Ochs, Jennie Strawn, and Tillie Smith. The small boy to the right is Victor Smith, a future chief burgess of Quakertown Borough.

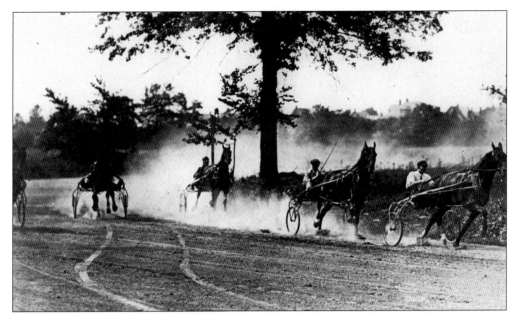

Harness racing events were part of the entertainment provided at the annual fair held at Lulu Park, now the location of the Quakertown Senior High School campus. Local jockeys and jockey wannabes competed for cash prizes. In 1900, the purse for the main horse race was $48, a goodly sum at the beginning of the 20th century.

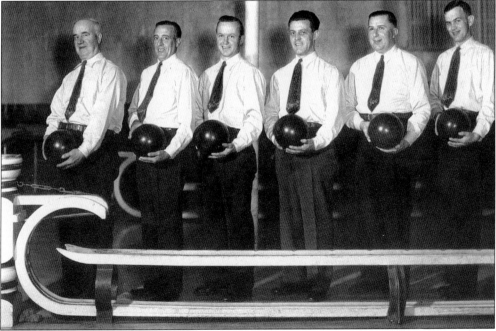

Members of the 1947 Owls bowling team pose for a picture in the bowling alley on Broad Street, in the building that formerly had been the location of the trolley barn. They are, from left to right, Bob Martin, Ray Wisler, Charlie Shinn, Bert Shinn, Roland (Joe) Schultz, and Bob Rapp. The Owls Social Club on Belmont Avenue closed in 1985 after approximately 60 years of activity.

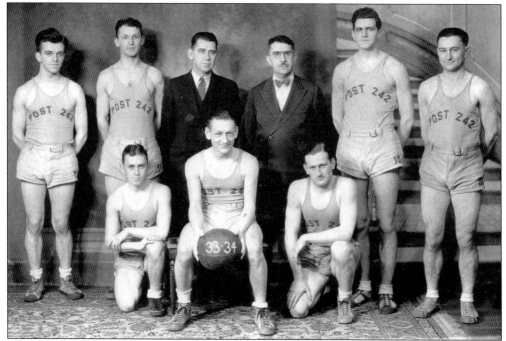

American Legion Post No. 242 was another social club that sponsored athletic teams. The court men on the 1933–1934 team are, from left to right, as follows: (front row) Bobby Moser, Paul Dietz, and Harvey Hartman; (back row) Paul Weber, Willard Moyer, manager Bill Bilger, coach Jacob Stoneback, Harlan Koder, and John Stockburger. The American Legion basketball teams played their games in the pavilion at the Bucks County Fairgrounds, at the Broad Theater, in the Goodwill Social Hall, and at the Moose Hall.

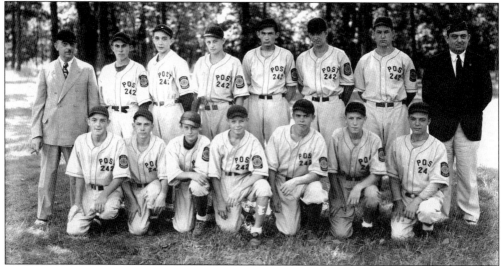

American Legion Post No. 242 has also sponsored baseball teams for nearly 70 years, beginning with this team in 1933. From left to right are the following: (front row) Mark Afflerbach, Tommy Fluck, "Honey" Fly, Johnny Smoll, Johnny Kemmerer, Wayne Harr, and Raymond Johnson; (back row) coach Jake Stoneback, Willard Fly, Walter Pearsall, Rich Lewis, Jerry Rosenberger, Lloyd Gross, Clyde Badman, and manager Roland C. Moeller.

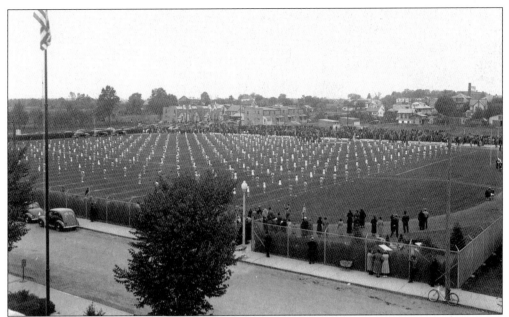

On Saturday, October 9, 1937, more than 1,300 people participated in a parade and athletic games when Quakertown High School's new $20,000 athletic field on Seventh Street was dedicated. More than 700 high school students gathered on the field for a display of calisthenics under the supervision of John O. Barth and Dorothy Hoyt. The main speakers were Gen. Smedley D. Butler, commander in the U.S. Marines in World War I, and Hon. Hiram H. Keller, president judge of Bucks County Courts.

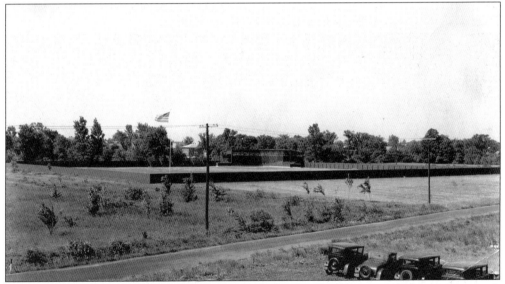

On Sunday, June 11, 1939, the new facility built for the Quakertown Athletic Association's East Penn League baseball team was dedicated as Memorial Park. Dr. Calvin Moyer presided over the festivities, and Pennsylvania attorney general Gordon Luckenbill gave the dedication address. The eight acres of land had been bought by the Quakertown Athletic Association from St. Isidore's Church. In 1945, the Quakertown Athletic Association turned the land and facilities over to the borough for $1.

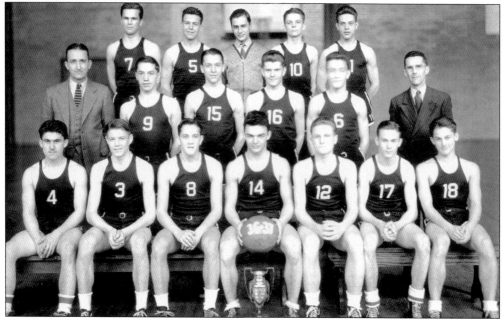

The 1936–1937 Quakertown High School boys' basketball team won the Bux-Mont championship, the first of three basketball championship teams coached by John O. Barth. From left to right are the following: (front row) Willard Farrel, John Smoll, Don Gerhab, Sterling Detweiler, Rich Panceygrau, Jim Wenhold, and Alton Fly; (middle row) coach John O. Barth, Earl Egner, William Feigley, Earl Hanselman, George Satek, and athletic director Jesse Cressman; (back row) Rich Long, Paul Heavener, Roscoe Jarrett, Paul Bitner, and William Buzby.

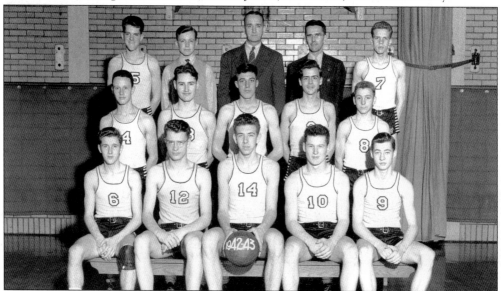

This 1942–1943 team was also led by Barth to the Bux-Mont championship. Pictured, from left to right, are the following: (front row) Bill Cauthorne, Leon Erdman, Bill Landis, Warren Gerhart, and Dick Davis; (middle row) Dick Shaw, Doug Kauffman, Bob Keller, Ken DeReiter, and Doug Shelly; (back row) Ken Martin, Harold Kachline, coach John O. Barth, athletic director Jesse Cressman, and Bob Gilbert.

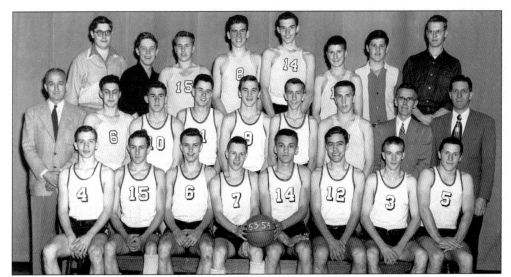

The 1953–1954 "never-say-die" team beat Pennridge in an exciting overtime win at Lehigh University's Grace Hall to give coach Barth his third title. From left to right are the following: (front row) Donald Knechel, Donald VanAuken, Robert Bealer, Harry Dietz, Jack Znotens, William Rosch, Kenneth Fly, and Tom Moyer; (middle row) coach John O. Barth, Rob Horne, Charles Kline, Elwood MacWhorter, Hal Fly, David Myers, Richard Kline, Jesse Cressman, and assistant coach Richard Wisneski; (back row) John Moyer, Leonard Myers, James Collins, William Hunscher, Theodore Bozarth, David Moyer, Richard Benner, and manager Donald Bourquin.

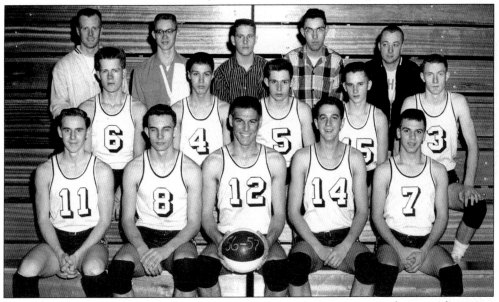

Under second-year head coach Don Young, the 1956–1957 Bux-Mont championship team defeated Neshaminy High School in a first-round playoff game at Abington. The Panthers lost 74-68 to Chester High School in a hard-fought, second-round playoff game at the Penn Palestra. Shown, from left to right, are the following: (front row) Rick Hilmer, Paul Bealer, Ed Becker, Ken Biehn, and John Detweiler; (middle row) Atis Lielmanis, Ken Benner, Norman Slotter, Galen Gerhart, and Rick Shutters; (back row) assistant coach Dick Bader, Ron Cassel, Ed Hacker, Wayne Mumbauer, and coach Don Young.

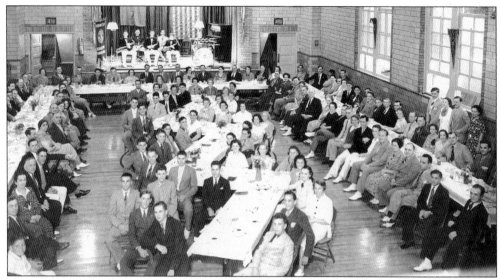

The 1930s were glory years for both the boys' and girls' Quakertown High School basketball teams. The Quakertown Kiwanis Club gave a testimonial dinner at the Moose Hall for the two teams, at which the two coaches, John O. Barth and Evelyn Hartman, were presented with gifts by members of their teams. The guest speakers that evening were two members of the Philadelphia Athletics American League baseball team, Lou Finney and Wally Moses.

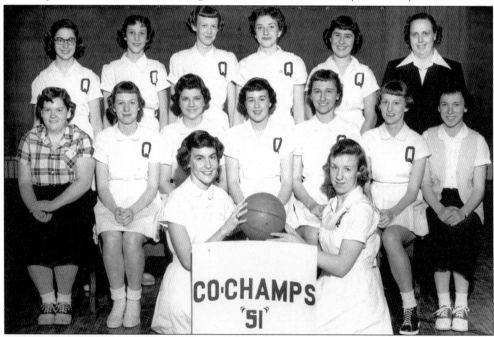

A Bux-Mont League ruling in 1951 mandated that all girls' basketball games be played during the day. This change did not keep coach Marian Afflerbach from leading the team to an 8-1 record, including a 76-26 triumph over Lansdale. From left to right are the following: (front row) co-captains Jacki Short and Joan Koehler; (middle row) K. Dietz, H. Dietz, J. Heimbach, H. Koder, L. Reese, M. Kneller, and P Horne; (back row) J. Stoneback, S. Hoffman, N. Smith, S. Neas, T. Moyer, and coach Afflerbach.

96

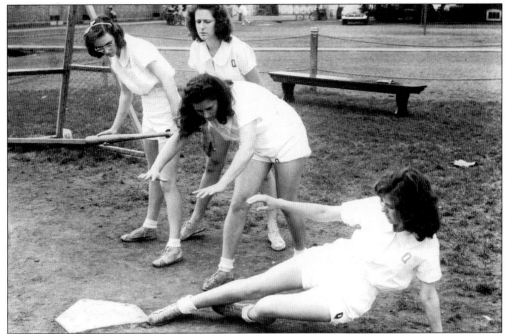

Quakertown High School science teacher and photography club advisor Warren Buck skillfully posed four members of the 1946 softball team for this "action" photograph. From left to right, they are Janet Wagner, Anna Crouthamel, Florence Dietz, and Josephine Sorbello. Perhaps Buck's skillful direction helped inspire Sorbello to pursue an acting career; she went on to appear in numerous movies and television programs under the name Jan Shepard. She is featured in chapter 9 of this book.

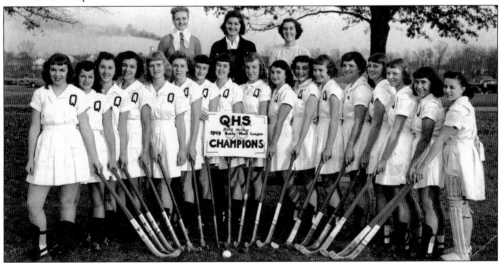

This proud 1949 group of Lady Panther athletes represents the first of two consecutive Bux-Mont League championship field hockey teams. From left to right are the following: (front row) Lorraine Loughridge, Wilma Hartman, Betty Trautman, Connie Jett, Lillian Rhoades, Barbara Bergman, Connie Lewis, Helen Koder, Joan Koehler, Sylvia Moyer, Audrey Newhard, Doris Stumb, Jessica Heimbach, Mary Kneller, Harriet Dietz, Thelma Moyer, and Fay Stull; (back row) Katherine White, coach Eleanor Pengelsi (Miss Aff was on a leave of absence), and Sylvia Harner.

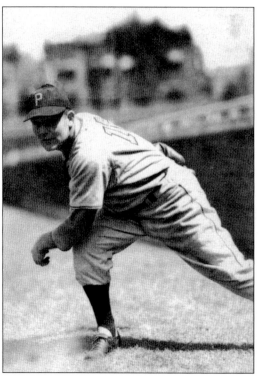

In the early 1930s, when Clyde Smoll attended Quakertown High School, baseball was truly the national pastime, so it was the big news when Smoll signed with the Detroit Tigers. After playing for a Tigers' Minor League team, the Atlanta Crackers, he joined the Philadelphia Phillies and appeared in 23 games for the local National League team as a relief pitcher. "Lefty" also pitched for the Baltimore Orioles, compiling a 19-17 won-lost record over three years. Smoll managed in the Cleveland Indians' farm system after he retired as a player.

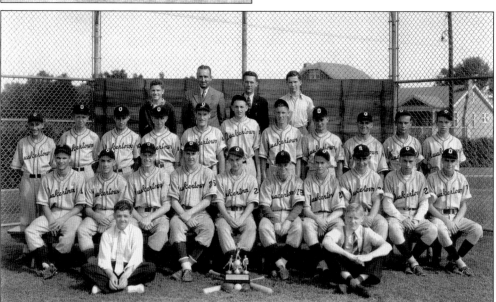

John O. Barth lead four consecutive Quakertown High School baseball teams to championships in the 1930s, the last being this 1938 team. From left to right are the following: (first row) two unidentified; (second row) Richard Long, Earl Long, John Smoll, Stan Slotter, Alton Fly, Ken Scheetz, Jim Wenhold, Ed Funk, Fred Romig, and Robert Ahlum; (third row) Arlington Lewis, Cliff Kachline, Ralph Buzby, Red Schaffer, Art Jenkins, Leroy Wagner, Earl Gross, Art Kaiser, John Strawsnyder, Willard Grube, and Willard Landis; (fourth row) manager Charles Stever, coach John O. Barth, athletic director Jesse Cressman, and manager Leon Nace.

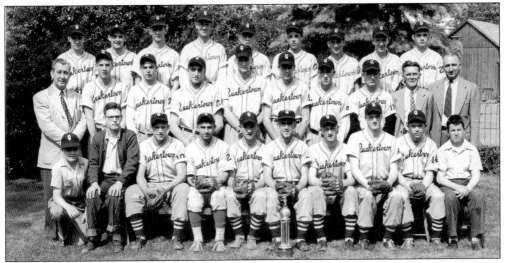

Coach Barth led his fifth Panther baseball team to a Bux-Mont championship in 1950. Pictured, from left to right, are the following: (front row) manager Earl Arn, manager Walter Long, Robert Koehler, Gerald Mayer, Charles Egner, Jim "Spider" Myers, Dick Hillegas, Dick Miller, Joe Yerkes, and Joe Willauer; (middle row) assistant coach Cliff Reese, Walter Hunsberger, Barry Grim, Willard Rosenberger, George Barringer, Bob Detweiler, Ray Gerhart, Bill Cramp, athletic director Jesse Cressman, and coach J.O. Barth; (back row) Ronald Heller, Larry Grim, John Moyer, Forrest Kaufman, Robert Slotter, Steward Powell, Clyde Rigel, Jack Slotter, and Richard Hostetter.

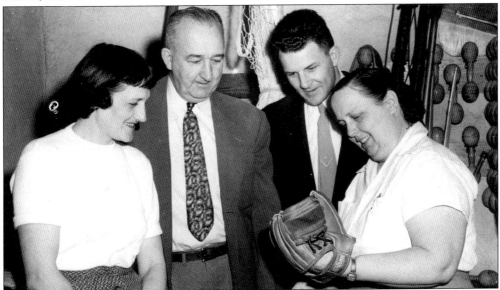

Many Quakertown athletes, from the 1930s to the present day, have benefited from the leadership provided by these teachers who also served as coaches. Alice Moyer, at the far left, coached several junior high school teams. Next is John O. Barth, whose coaching spanned three decades and whose success is well documented on these pages. Third from the left is Paul Barndt, who still coaches Quakertown High School track and football teams. Finally, Marian Afflerbach, also known as "Miss Aff," was the field hockey, softball, and girls' basketball coach in the middle part of the 20th century.

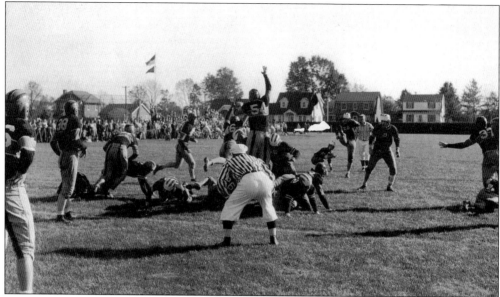

Paul "Moose" Barndt, future coach, teacher, and administrator, kicks a field goal during a game played in 1945 on Alumni Field. The following year, the stadium seating was increased and lights were installed, and all football games except the Thanksgiving Day game were played at night. Holding for Moose is Eugene Lang. Blocking are Mike Contros (No. 16) and Bob Schlicter (No. 8).

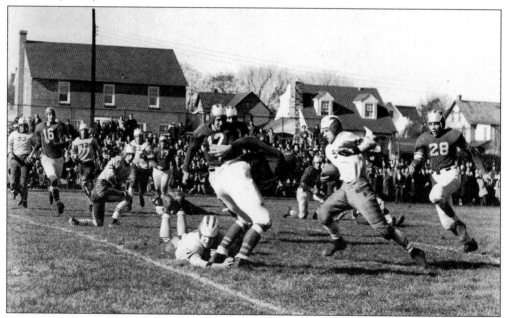

Herman Faul manages a short gain against Sell-Perk High School in the 1946 Thanksgiving Day game played on Alumni Field. Also involved in the play are Dick Neubert (No. 33), John Stahr (No. 12), John Strawn (No. 23), and Bill Lewis (No. 17). Since 1933, this traditional Thanksgiving rivalry has been held on alternate years at the Quakertown and Sell-Perk (now Pennridge) football fields. The series has included many memorable games, including the 2000 record-setting six-overtime game won by Quakertown 52-45.

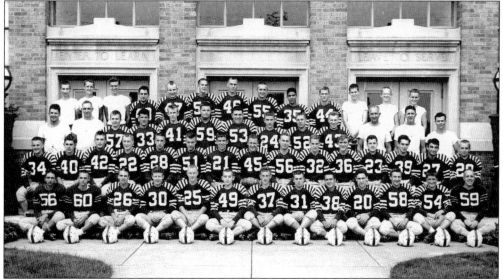

The first Quakertown High School Bux-Mont League football championship was won by this 1954 team. From left to right are the following: (first row) G. Banas, E. Noll, J. Detweiler, W. Auckland, R. Shutters, M. Tirjan, J. Hoffert, D. Hillegass, K. Rush, A. Schmeck, O. Mastin, D. Moyer, and R. Pearson; (second row) Z. Papciak, C. Kline, J. Znotens, D. Rosenberger, R. Kline, R. Bealer, W. Hunscher, T. Moyer, W. Landes, H. Brown, H. Fly, E. MacWhorter, R. Balliet, G. Contros, and R. Benner; (third row) coach Barndt, coach Martin, C. Texter, R. Benner, R. Swartz, R. Richmond, R. Collier, P King, J. Collins, H. Dietz, coach Barth, coach Wisneski, and coach Fluck; (fourth row) R. Trumbauer, A. Treffinger, K. Fretz, F. Tarantino, D. Fischer, K. Biehn, E. Becker, R. Landgreen, J. Jett, T. Dodson, G. Noble, J. Bockius, and R. Hilmer.

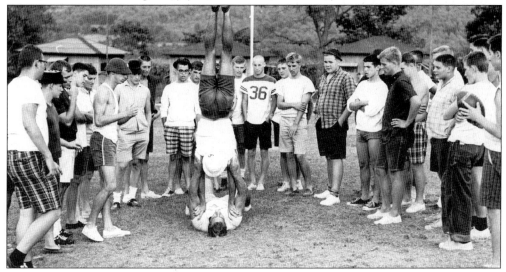

Before the 1964 football season, Quakertown High School players retreated to Camp Dent in the Pocono Mountains to escape the Quakertown August heat. Between drills and play lessons, a couple of the players squeezed in time for some showing off. The group watching them includes Larry Bobiak, Jeff Johnston, Tom Hangey, Jim Griffith, Steve Swartley, Mike Clisham, Ed Mettin, Bill Hafler, Jeff Harr, Dave Edge, Dave Robinson, Jim Fosbenner, Art Booth, Ken Williams, and Bob Colodonato.

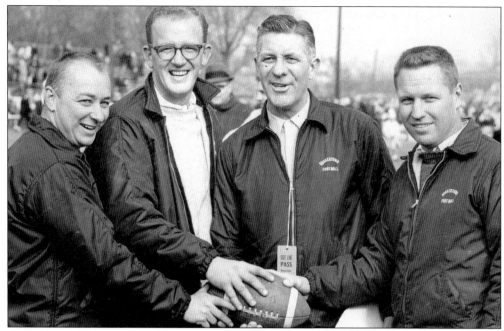

Quakertown High School's 1965 football coaching staff—from left to right, Don Young, Ray Ely, Dick Wisneski, and Doug Peiffer—have a lot to smile about. The Panthers have just defeated Pennridge 13-6 on Thanksgiving Day to win the Bux-Mont League football championship with a 9-1 overall record. The victory over the Rams was especially sweet; the last Thanksgiving Day victory for the Panthers in the classic series had been in 1960.

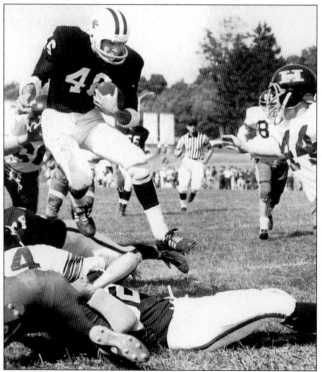

Ken Schroy goes over the top to make a gain against Hatboro-Horsham during the 1970 Quakertown Panther football season. Schroy played both offense and defense that season and led the team to a Bux-Mont League championship. Schroy played college football at the University of Maryland, where he started on defense and was honored twice as Atlantic Coast Conference player of the week. Schroy went on to play with the NFL New York Jets as a defensive back and special teams player.

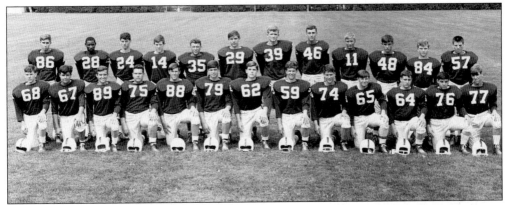

These sophomore football players on the 1968 Quakertown High School football team were developing skills that, as seniors, would earn them the 1970 Bux-Mont championship. They are, from left to right, as follows: (front row) Dan Fluck, Eugene Orzel, Tom Fosbenner, Dennis Hallman, Tom Koehler, Todd Youngblood, Ken Eisenhart, Kevin Bauman, Tom Schlicter, Dale Clymer, Cliff Mease, John Eisenhart, and Keith Dieterly; (back row) Richard Neiman, Ed Powell, Alan Hillegass, Ken Stoudt, Ronald Schulberger, Ken Slotter, Jeff Barndt, Jeff Schroy, John Gross, Steve Fischer, Robin Luppinacci, and Zachary Ewaniuk.

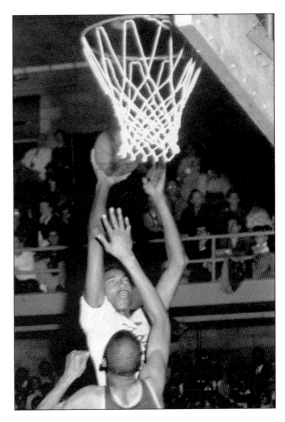

NBA great Wilt Chamberlain played for the semiprofessional Quakertown Fays during the 1954–1955 Big Nine Conference season. Chamberlain was a senior at Overbrook High School in Philadelphia. The Pennsylvania Athletic Association did not at that time have jurisdiction over the city schools, so Chamberlain could play professionally without losing his eligibility. In 15 games for the Fays, who played their home games at Benner Hall in Richlandtown, Wilt averaged 53.9 points. He is seen here at Allentown's Rockne Hall shooting over 6-foot 11-inch Andy Maddox, who had previously played for the Harlem Globetrotters.

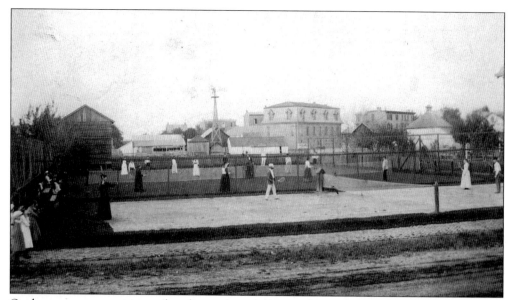

Quakertown community members have a long tradition of actively participating in athletic and recreational activities. These tennis courts (above), which were near Third and Juniper Streets during the 1890s, and the storefront YMCA office (below), which was at Third and Broad Streets in the late 1960s, are earlier representations of this involvement. The YMCA has greatly expanded its operations since being in that storefront office and plans to open state-of-the-art facilities in the near future. This will help sustain our long and distinguished tradition of scholastic and community athletic involvement.

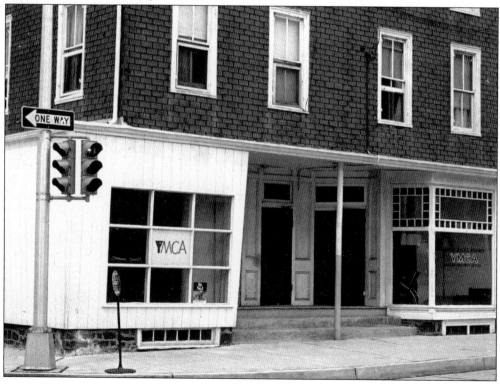

Nine

ENJOYING ARTS AND LEISURE

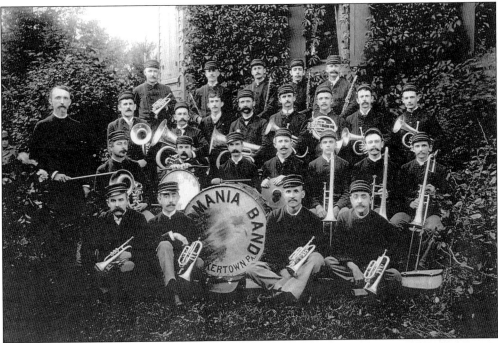

The Quakertown Band had its beginning on February 22, 1877, when 23 men met in Aaron B. Walp's shoe factory on East Broad Street. They were determined to create music. Seventeen of this group were shoemakers by trade. They chose Peter Smith, a cornetist, as their first leader. Because they used a complete set of Lenhardt German silver instruments, they adopted the name of Citizens Silver Cornet Band. In the early 1880s, because of style changes, they acquired new instruments, which were made of brass. Since the band's name was no longer appropriate, they chose the title Germania Band in 1883. This title fell out of favor, however, in World War I; therefore, the group settled simply upon the Quakertown Band. The band is pictured as it looked in 1893. From left to right are the following: (first row) Daniel Hoffman, Peter Moyer, George Harding, and William C. Hillegas; (second row) Rev. J.F. Ohl, Charles Walp, George Weitz, Morris Krauss, Oswin Moll, Charles Schoup, Romanus Miller, and James Bortz; (third row) Andrew Hoffman, William Bleam, Lewis E. Bleam, Edward Stoudt, Charles Rhoades, John Moyer, Albanus Freed, and Edward Mininger; (fourth row) William Benner, Charles Wolmer, Curt Hallman, Harry Moyer, and Tilghman Walp.

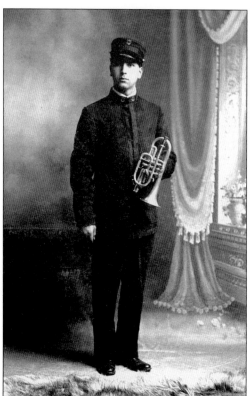

Lewis Pfaff, director of the Quakertown Band from 1913 to 1925, grew up with the band and had been a member since 1898. An accomplished cornetist, he received a bid to join the U.S. Marine Corps Band. By choosing not to become a professional musician, he stayed in town and served as a dynamic leader of the Quakertown Band.

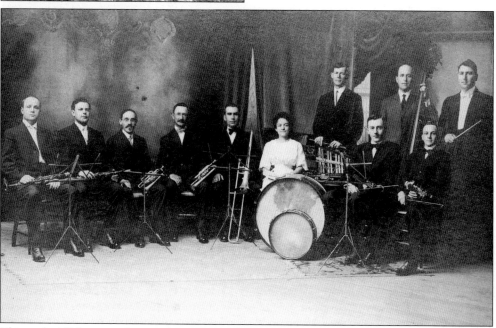

This early-1920s musical group features members of the Pfaff's Orchestra. Sitting, from left to right, are Winfield Arn, ? Hillegass, Abraham Shelly, Harvey Price, ? Schoup, Bertha Hallman, Robert B. Henry, and Norman Frank. Standing, from left to right, are Francis Rantz, Worman Shelly, and conductor Lewis Pfaff.

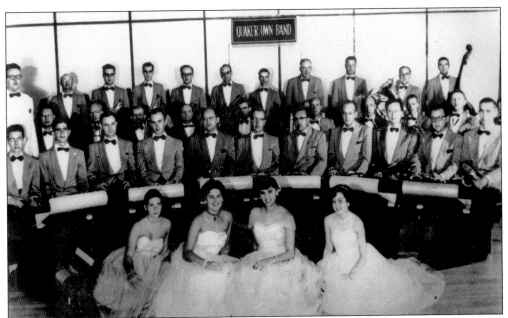

In 1957, the Quakertown Band was popular for its smooth sound under the direction of Ralph R. Moyer. Moyer, wearing white, is standing on the extreme left. Women soloists seated in the front are, from left to right, Arlene Bickel, Joan Fretz Vogt, Shirley Helm Rupert, and Norma Frank Donner.

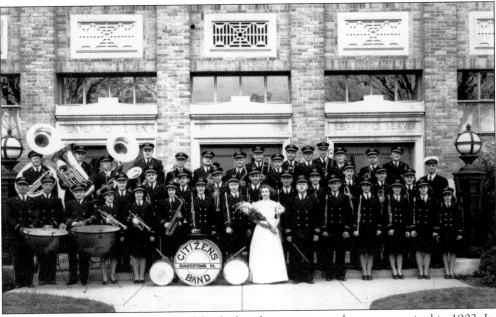

The Citizens Band, a marching band fond of performing in parades, was organized in 1902. Its first conductor was Harry Moyer. Worman M. Shelly served as conductor for 38 years. Its last leader before it disbanded was Richard Nase. The band performed its final annual concert on March 31, 1968, in the auditorium of Quakertown Community High School. In this 1948 picture, the band is standing in front of the entrance to the former junior-senior high school on Seventh Street.

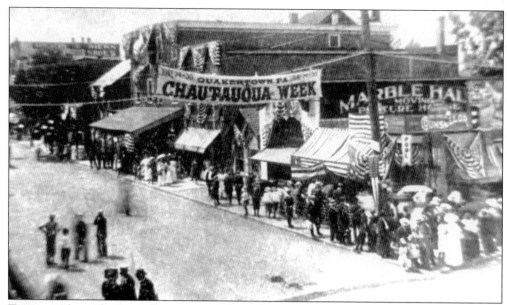

Townspeople enthusiastically participated in the annual Chautauqua Week activities that came to town from 1912 to 1927. Frank Ball is credited with launching the project locally. Chautauqua offerings included lectures, recitals, plays, pageants, and concerts. The tents to house the event were pitched first at Fifth and Juniper Streets, and later at Sixth and Juniper Streets. In this view of downtown, the street banner announces Chautauqua Week for June 1914. To the right can be seen Marble Hall (on West Broad Street), which was Quakertown's first motion picture theater. Admission was 5¢.

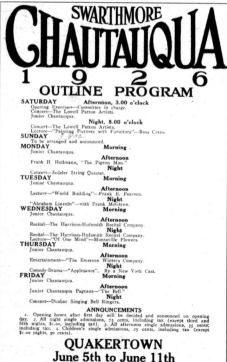

This program, dated June 5–11, 1926, illustrates the variety of educational and cultural offerings of Chautauqua, an institution originating in New York, in 1874. Other communities throughout the United States were inspired to form local Chautauqua and engaged authors, explorers, musicians, and actors to instruct and entertain. Fred A. Krauss wrote in the *Free Press*, "It [Chautauqua] led us to noble thoughts and aspirations."

With the demise of the *Tripper* in 1929, trolley cars were no longer stored and repaired at the Traction Company next to Klein's House Furnishings Store on East Broad Street. The building then housed the Broad movie house, which showed early silent films. It was also used to hold high school graduations because then the school had no auditorium. Later, it became a bowling alley. Today, it serves as an antiques shop.

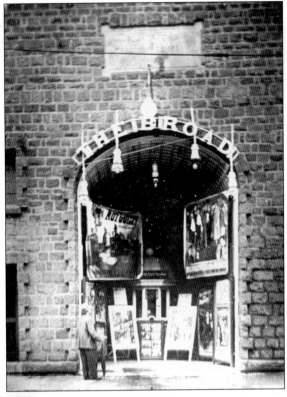

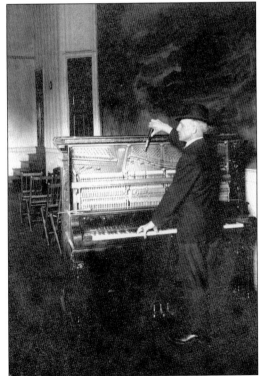

This nattily dressed gentleman is tuning the piano at the Broad, on East Broad Street. It was customary for a pianist to play appropriate music as background for silent films. Imagine the excitement in the Broad when the pianist played an accompaniment to *The Hunchback of Notre Dame*, starring Lon Chaney.

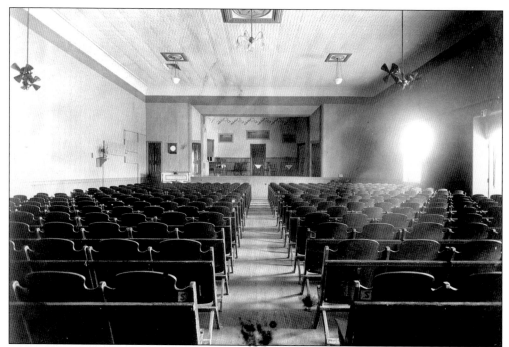

This interior view of the Broad features Spartan auditorium seats and a stage with a simple set for a play.

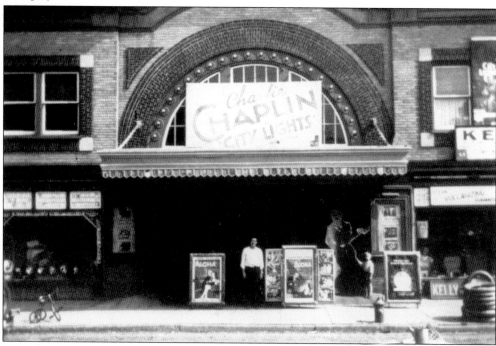

Generations of families were entertained by movies and shows at the Palace Theatre, west of the railroad tracks on West Broad Street. In 1971, the theater closed and the building became the retail store for Dimmig Electric. At the time this picture was taken, people could see Charlie Chaplin in *City of Lights* and another film called *Aloha*.

Mrs. Leo Minnucci, who formed a dance team with her husband, appears in this portrait much as she must have looked in May 1926, when the couple danced at a Saturday matinee and evening show on the stage at the Palace Theatre.

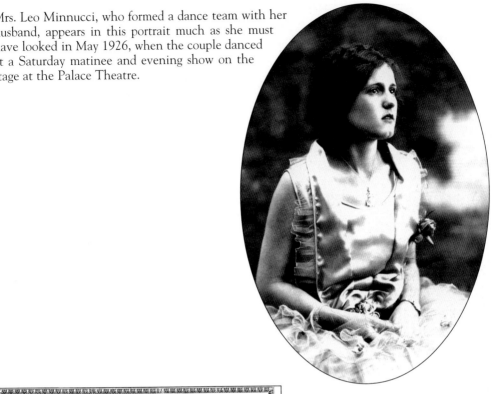

The Great Spectacular Fire Play

The Fire Brigade

Bobby Lamkens, Manager and Director

Thursday and Friday, Feb. 28 and 29
Palace Theatre (1924) Quakertown, Pa.

Benefit of Quakertown Fire Company. No. 1

CAST OF CHARACTERS	
Captain Paul Williams	Norman R. Frank
Chas. Branden, Chief	R. E. Strunk
Patrick O'Flaherty, Foreman	Bobby Lamkens
Jake Parsons, an old timer	Earl Allison
Tommy Wilcox, Nozzleman	William Schissler
Joseph Andrews	Warren Fluck
Bob, the news boy	Wilson Smith
Dustie Rhonds	R. E. Strunk
The Ghost	By Him Self
Officer Pullem	R. LaMar Fretz
The Merry Widow	Mildred Moyer
Edith Brandon	Laura Heimbach
Polly Weston	Kathryn Reider
Little Dot	Elvetta Reider
Dot (10 years later)	Mercy Smith
Dooley Girl	Hazel Smoll
Dooley Girl	Dorothy Fly

Assisted by 16 firemen dressed in full uniform in full action on the stage.

Orchestra

SPECIALTY LIST
"My Tommy Boy,"
Kathryn Reider and William Schissler
(Published by G. W. Setchell, New York and Boston)
Firemen's Grand Chorus Opening Act II.
"When We Ran with the Old Machine,"
Earl Allison and Chorus
(Specially composed and arranged for this production by Bobby Lamkens.)
"The Man Who Fights," Wm. Schissler and Chorus
(Published by the Paul Dresser Pub. Co., 51 West 28th Street, N. Y.)
Grand Chorus Opening Act III
"Dooley Girls" . . . . . . Hazel Smoll and Dorothy Fly
"Oh! What a Lovely Dream," (Hobo Spec.)
R. LaMar Fretz
(Published by Shapiro, Bernstein & Co., 45 West 28th Street, N.Y.)
"If I Should" (duet from "The Runaways")
William Schissler and Kathryn Reider
(Published by M. Witmark & Sons, New York, Boston, Chicago, San Francisco, London.)

SYNOPSIS ACT I.	SYNOPSIS ACT III.
The Home of Widow McGowen.	(The Firemen's Annual Tournament)
The Murder.	The Picnic Party.
The Firemen's Oath.	The Attempt to Murder Dot.
"Arrest that Man."	"Hang Him!" "Lynch Him!"
	Tableau.

SYNOPSIS ACT II.	SYNOPSIS ACT IV.
(Early evening—10 years later)	(Early Evening—Three Months Later.)
Quakertown Fire Co., No. 1.	The Home of Widow McGowen.
Firemen's Grand Opening Chorus.	The Great Fire Scene.
(Firemen and Old Engine all ready for action).	Quakertown Fire Co., No. 1 to the rescue.
The attempt to steal of papers.	The Heroic Life Net Leap.
The Widdy on the warpath.	"Turn the Hose on Me."
"There's Something Doing."	

Curtain Rises at 8.15   Pfaff's Orchestra

Who says that our forebears believed in all work and no play? This program for *The Fire Brigade* illustrates that they knew how to have fun at the same time they acquired funds for the benefit of the Quakertown Fire Company. The mayhem took place on the stage of the Palace Theatre in 1924.

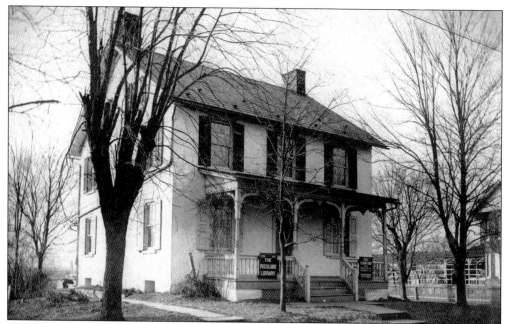

The Richland Library Company, at 44 South Main Street, was organized in 1788. It is the third oldest library in Bucks County and the seventh oldest in the United States. Until 1911, when it was moved into the building pictured, the library collection was housed in private dwellings. Its contents are an interesting mix of rare and original volumes joined by contemporary technology to preserve collections and facilitate research. The library's 1795 charter has been conserved and framed and is on display in the library. Family records and genealogical information are safely stored in the library.

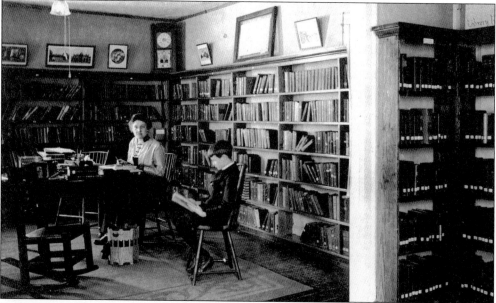

Freda Haring, librarian of the Richland Library, is seated at the still-used round table in the main circulation room of the library. The boy who is reading is Dan Strawn, who later served for more than 50 years as treasurer of the library. The picture was taken *c.* 1910.

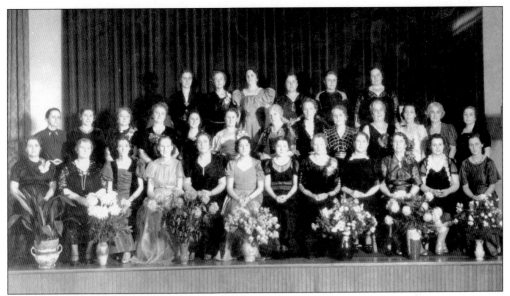

The Quakertown Woman's Club, organized in 1911 and still active today, had a large chorus in the 1930s. These members are, from left to right, as follows: (front row) Minnie Keller, four unidentified guests, Polly Leinbach, Hazel Krauss, ? Dick, Olive Henry, Ida Jane Meredith, Ellen Hinkel, and Grace Weber; (middle row) Gladys Feigley, Ernestine Thornton, Mary Benner, Ella Meredith, Helen Mood, Margarette Kooker, ? Rufe, Louise McGovern, Minnie Hixson, ? Kirkpatrick, Ruth Baker, ? Muehlhauser, and ? Pease; (back row) Edith Weamer, Gertrude Biehn, Velma Rosenberger, ? Diehl, Ivy Erdman, and ? Clymer.

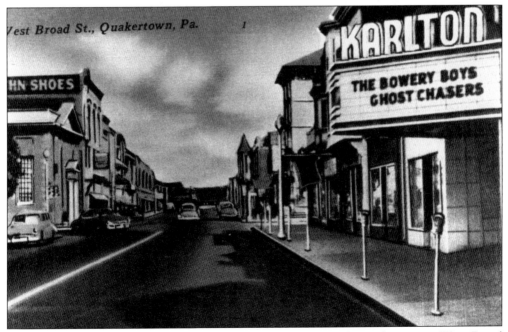

Merged with its sister theater (the Palace) after 1931, the Karlton Theatre, on West Broad Street next to the *Free Press* building, closed its doors in 1967 after providing entertainment for many. Today, the site is occupied by retail shops and a cafe.

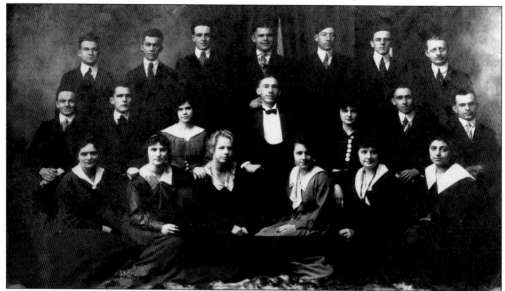

Pictured *c.* 1915–1916 are the members of the North Penn Dramatics Club. They are, from left to right, as follows: (front row) Florence Kilmer Surgeson, Edna Biehn Kilmer, Ella Moyer, Laura Heimbach Louis, Pearl Heimbach Hittinger, and Kate Lewis Keller; (middle row) Norman Frank, Jesse Cressman, Miriam Gehringer Sattler, Eugene Keller, Alma Bartholomew Biehn, Milton Biehn, and Harry Steigner; (back row) Francis Nadig, Ralston Fluck, Vincent Conway, Harold Texter, John Harr, Joseph Neidig, and Henry Detweiler.

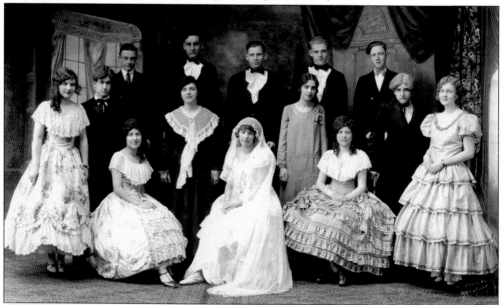

In 1928, the junior class of Quakertown High School performed the play *Smilin' Through*. Seated to the left of the "bride" is Jeanette Benson. Seated to the right of the "bride" is Hazel Smoll Slotter. Standing to the extreme left are Kathryn Reider Fretz and Ernest Hendricks. Standing to the right of the "bride" is Marguerite Neal Rush. Standing behind Rush is August Wackerman. The "old man" standing second from the right is Wayne Steeley. The other cast members are unidentified.

114

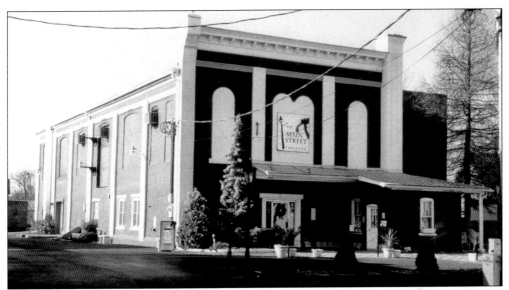

Looking at its attractive blue-and-white facade, today's theatergoers at the Main Street Theatre might not guess the varied uses to which this building has been put over the years. A nonprofit organization owned and operated by its governing board of directors, the Main Street Theatre has, since 1994, brought drama, comedy, and music to an area previously denied live professional theater. The building on South Main Street was originally built as the livery stable for the nearby Red Lion Inn. For many years, it was used as a factory.

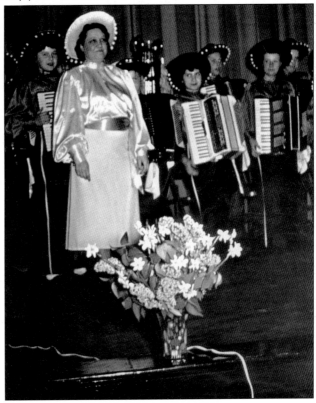

The Maccabees organization sponsored an accordion band in the early 1950s. Featured on stage are, from left to right, Nancy Wieder Roberts, Sylvia Wrigley, Josephine Galluppi, John Landgreen, Nancy Fulmer Percival, and Dale Sine.

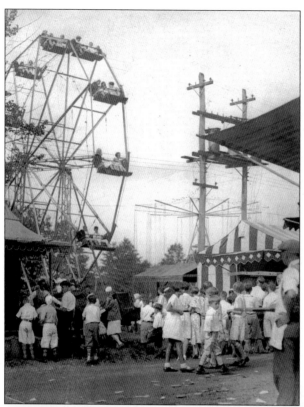

Open land just off Park Avenue stretching from what is now Third to Ninth Streets, formerly known as Lotts Woods, became the home of Lulu Park, which opened in 1883. The park provided a variety of entertainment and hosted an annual fair that included harness racing, dancing, an exposition and midway, carnival rides, food, and music.

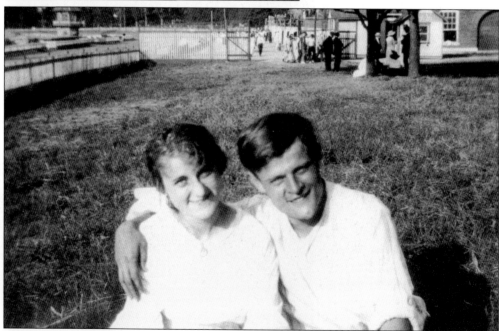

Sally Graff and brother Louis Graff are enjoying a few quiet moments away from the noise and activity of Lulu Park, seen in the background. Their visit to the park was probably in the early 1920s. The Quakertown Community Senior High School complex now occupies this area.

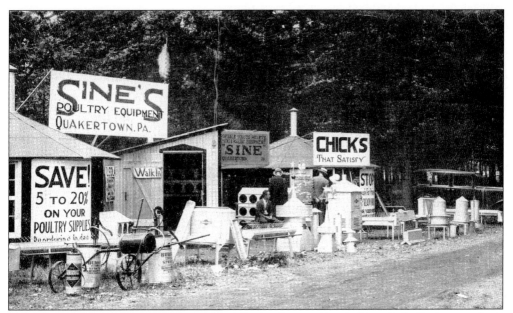

One of the popular features at the annual Bucks County Fair held in Lulu Park was a long avenue of exhibitions provided by shopkeepers, businessmen, agencies, and services. In this photograph, Alvin C. Sine, a distributor for chicks and poultry equipment, displayed samples of his products, which were housed at his business on North Hellertown Avenue. Sometimes, exhibitors would distribute free souvenirs such as yardsticks or potholders.

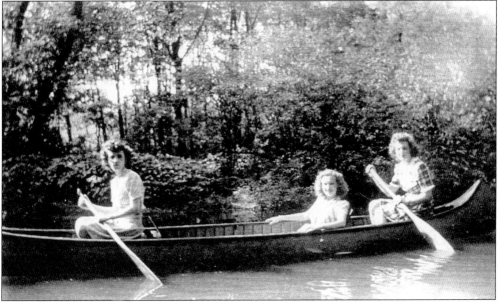

The young girls enjoying a canoe ride are Shirley Koder Neubert, on the left, and her sisters. Reminiscing about the Tohickon Creek, Shirley wrote, "Leaving the swimming and boat rental area we paddled under the old iron bridge up the creek. We passed concrete pillars now only a reminder of the bridge for the Q and E Railroad, for some forgotten reason still called the dinky. I had often heard that the dinky was a favorite spot for some of the older boys for skinny-dipping. Of course, I never tried to find out if this was true."

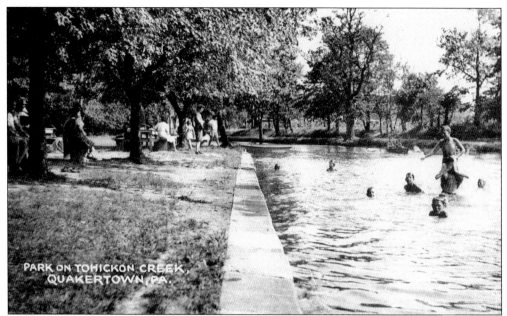

Until Eichner's Grove lost its appeal after the conclusion of World War II, when cars and gasoline became available for migration to modern pools and more sophisticated parks, Eichner's Grove offered swimming and boating in the summer and ice-skating in the winter. John Eichner operated his grove along the banks of the Tohickon Creek at the end of Tohickon Avenue.

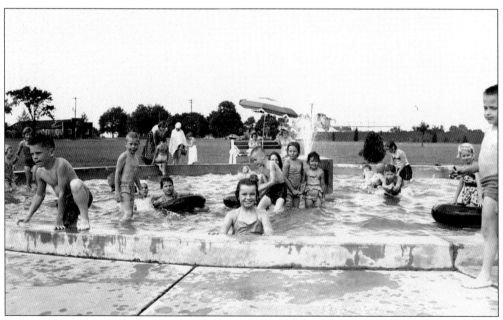

For many years before the construction of the Quakertown swimming pool, youngsters enjoyed splashing in this wading pool in Memorial Park on Mill Street. A gift of the Rotary Club, the wading pool was part of the summer recreation program directed by Richard E. Strayer and was always supervised by teachers. In this 1954 photograph, the girl in the foreground, looking at the camera, is Lorraine Maugle.

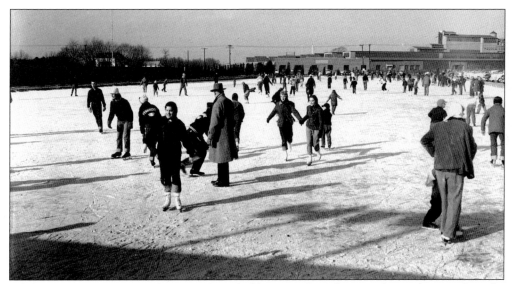

When winter temperatures drop, young and old put on their skates and join the crowd on the skating pond at Fourth and Mill Streets. In this view taken in 1953, the camera was aimed toward Mill Street where the Krupp Foundry, formerly the Hajoca, was located. Fourth Street is to the right of the picture.

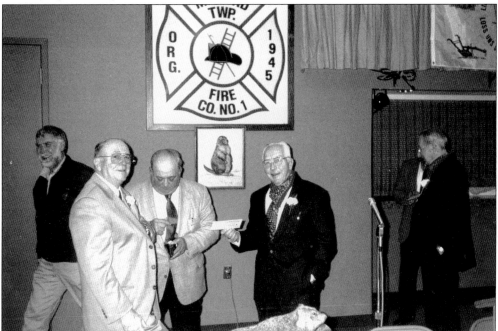

Members of Grundsow Lodge Nummer Fiere on Da Daheck (Number Four on the Tohickon) included, from left to right, an unidentified man, Orville Miller, Isaac Geissinger, Arlington Lewis, and Warren Buck. Lewis served as haaptman (leader) of this local lodge, which is one of 17 in eastern Pennsylvania whose purpose is to preserve and perpetuate the Pennsylvania German culture and dialect. This local lodge has been active since its founding in 1949 by Henry C. Detweiler, who "won seven lying contests" at annual Grundsow meetings, according to lodge records.

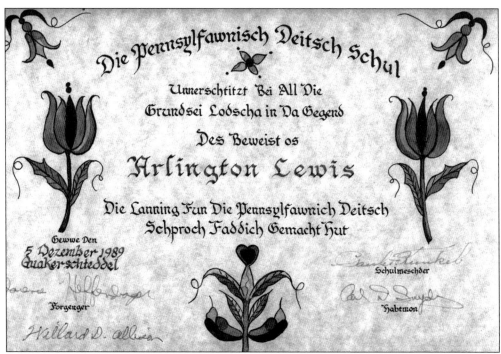

Die Pennsylfawnisch Deitsch Schul

Unnerschtitzt Bei All Die
Grundsei Lodscha in Da Gegend

Des Beweist os

Arlington Lewis

Die Lanning Fun Die Pennsylfawnich Deitsch
Schproch Faddich Gemacht Hut

Gewwe Den
5 Dezember 1989
Quakerschteddel

Vorgenger

Schulmeschder

Habtmon

Reproduced here is the diploma earned by Arlington Lewis for completing a 16-week course in the Pennsylvania German dialect. The course was given at Kutztown University in association with the Pennsylvania German Cultural Heritage Center and Museum. Lewis perpetuates the knowledge of the dialect by teaching courses at the public library and in the Adult Evening School Program. The heart and tulip motif on this diploma represents the skills and contributions of the Pennsylvania Germans in the field of arts and crafts.

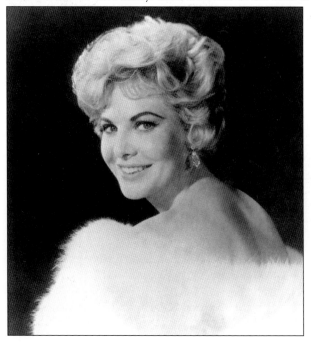

Jan Shepard, better known as Jo (Josephine) Sorbello in her Quakertown High School years, followed her dream to Hollywood and became an actress in motion pictures and television. She appeared in 8 movies, several features for television, 6 series, and more than 90 television shows. She made 2 movies with Elvis Presley, including *King Creole*. A few of the television shows in which she performed were *Perry Mason*, *The Loretta Young Show*, *Bonanza*, *Wyatt Earp*, and *Fireside Theatre*. Today, she is retired and lives in North Hollywood with her husband, Ray Boyle.

Ten
REMEMBERING UNIQUE
INDIVIDUALS

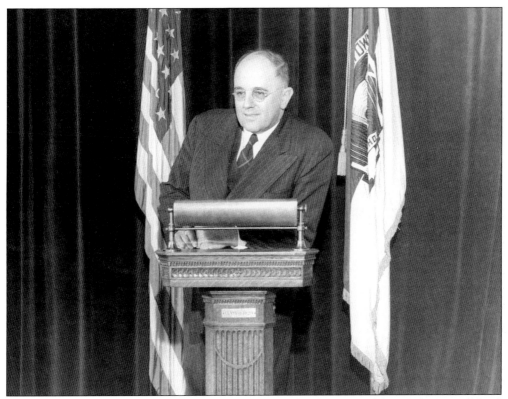

Joseph S. Neidig (1898–1958) was instrumental in the development of the Quakertown School District. During his leadership as superintendent of the district from 1924 until his death in 1958, he planned for the construction of major buildings. In 1929, he supervised the building of the former junior-senior high school on Seventh Street, now Quakertown Elementary. In 1956, he directed the construction of Quakertown Community Senior High School, at 600 Park Avenue. In 1958, shortly before his death, Neidig Elementary School was dedicated to him as a tribute to his faithful services to his hometown for the major part of his life. Neidig was a graduate of Quakertown High School, Muhlenberg College, and the University of Pennsylvania and was a member of Phi Beta Kappa. Having earned respect across the state and the nation, he was frequently called upon as an educational consultant.

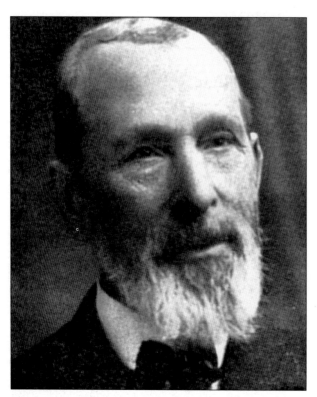

Aaron B. Walp (1828–1922), who led a long and active life in business and community service, joined his father in manufacturing boots and shoes in a factory at 122 East Broad Street. An original director of Quakertown National Bank, he later served as vice president for many years and was also a charter member and director of the Quakertown Trust Company. He was a member of the Quakertown Borough Council and helped organize the Quakertown Water Company. Active in the work of Trinity Lutheran Church, he served in its Sunday school for 70 years.

Dr. Joseph G. Thomas (1830–1908) was a prominent citizen, doctor, and financier who served as the first president of the Quakertown National Bank. After completing medical school and setting up a practice, he saw military action in the Civil War and was injured in combat. After the war, he resumed his medical practice. Thomas accumulated land, helped organize the Quakertown Masonic Lodge in 1872, and became a state senator in 1878.

Frank Ball (1853–1929) was the promoter and first president of a unique educational and cultural event, Chautauqua. Through his perseverance, Chautauqua visited Quakertown every summer from 1912 to 1927. He was active in additional community projects. A leader in the study of nature, he served as president of the Bucks County Natural Science Association. He was president of the Quakertown Building and Loan Association, treasurer of the Union Cemetery Association, an official of the Richland Horse and Insurance Company, a school director, and a respected member of the Society of Friends.

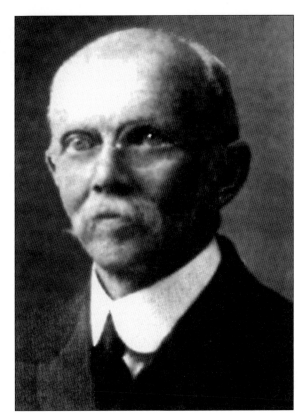

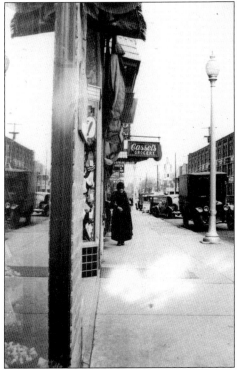

Strolling east on West Broad Street is Quakertown's famous itinerant, Alice Reiner. Born near Milford Square in 1870, Reiner began wandering at age 27, having left home after feuding with her parents over a suitor. In her black dress and battered hat, carrying all her belongings in a burlap bag, she walked the roads for 50 years, looking for a meal and a place to sleep. With Quakertown as her center, she walked in an approximately 40-mile radius. She was killed accidentally by an automobile in 1947. This picture was taken c. 1931.

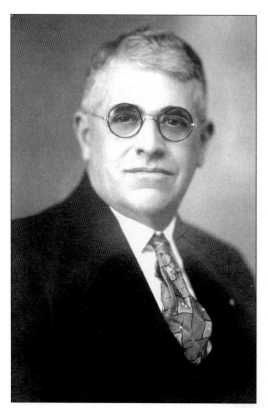

Edward W. Knauss (1870–1936) founded the Knauss Meat Processing and Packing Company in 1902, with a retail store at 103 East Broad Street and an abattoir, meatpacking, and wholesale house on East Broad Street near the borough limits. Knauss was also a director of Best Made Silk Hosiery. He married Ella Saylor, and their children were William E., who carried on the Knauss business, Mae (Mrs. Paul Deaterly), and Martha (Mrs. Ray Peters.)

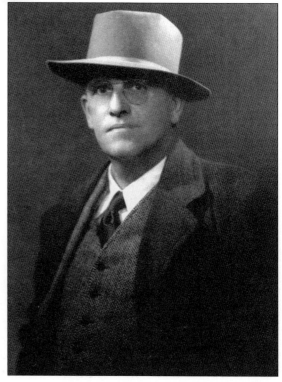

William E. Knauss (1896–1949) joined his father's meat-processing company in 1916. After much experimentation, he perfected a process for producing home-style curing on a commercial scale, enabling the company to expand production and increase its volume of business. William married Florence Tice in 1920. Their son, Donald T., took over the business in 1948.
E. William, son of Donald and Ruth Willauer Knauss, entered the business in 1968. E. William's son, Troy Knauss, leads the company today. He is the fifth-generation Knauss leading a company that has completed 100 years of business.

Florence Tice (1897–1985), who later became Mrs. William E. Knauss, was a keen observer who wrote interesting journals treasured by her family. After graduating from Swarthmore College, she became one of four teachers on the staff of Quakertown High School. She met her future husband when she chaperoned a high school dance attended by her students, twins Mae Knauss (Deaterly) and Martha Knauss (Peters), and their older brother, William E. Knauss. (At age 69, Florence escorted her 15-year-old granddaughter, Susan, on an independent tour of Europe.)

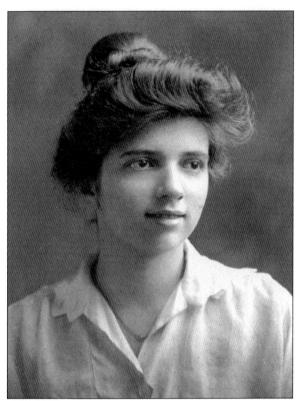

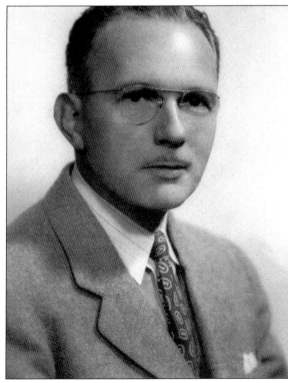

Dr. Raymond D. Tice (1899–1966), one of the community's foremost physicians, showed dedication to inhabitants for 43 years. He opened his medical practice in town, believing it was beneficial to practice in his hometown, where he knew most people and could converse in German and Pennsylvania German. At one time, he drove patients to and from Allentown Hospital. After the Quakertown Hospital opened in 1930, Tice bought the Gehman Nursing Home and turned it into the Tice Clinic, staffed by Dr. Raymond, Dr. Willard (Tice's brother), and Dr. Walter (Tice's son).

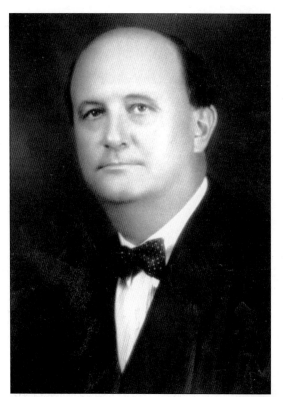

Charles M. Meredith (1874–1941), journalist and publisher, purchased the *Free Press* from its founder, Uriah S. Stauffer. Under his leadership, the *Free Press* became a weekly serving its community. Known for his wit, Meredith delivered more than 500 speeches in his career. A contemporary called his column a "window through which be observed the conduct of the world around him." He served as president of the National Editorial Association, vice president of the Pennsylvania Newspaper Publishers' Association, president of the Bucks-Montgomery Press League, and president of the Montgomery County Newspaper Association.

Charles M. Meredith Jr. (1904–1969) continued publishing the *Free Press* after his father. In 1955, he increased publication to five times a week and included local and world news. By converting the printing process, he greatly increased circulation. A graduate of the Wharton School of the University of Pennsylvania and Lehigh University, Meredith was active in the Bucks County Historical Society, the Pennsylvania Historical Society, the Pen and Pencil Club, and the Pennsylvania Newspaper Publishers' Association. His son, Charles M. Meredith III, continued publishing the *Free Press* into the late 1990s.

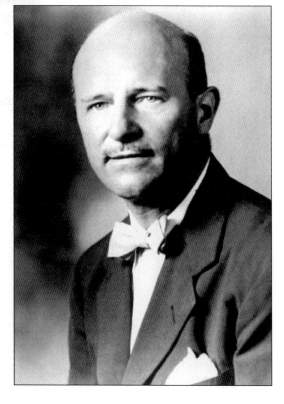

Laura S. Weinberger (1867–1963) came out of retirement at age 76 to teach high school science during World War II. The Class of 1947 dedicated its yearbook to her with these appropriate words: "Under her guidance we received, not only the rudiments of science, but also the zeal to learn, the desire for knowledge, and the basis for appreciation of the finer things in life. She has all the characteristics of an inspiring teacher; she possesses an indefinable quality of youth, a talent for refreshing wit, and an unusual zest for living."

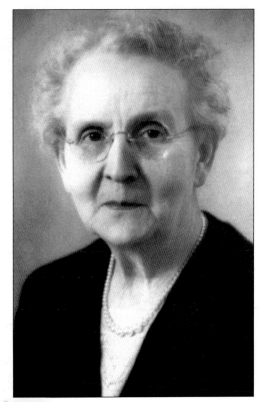

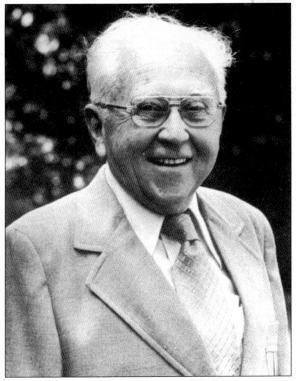

Alfred Johnson (1900–1984), also known as "Mr. Hospital," served as general chairman of the 1977 building fund campaign, which exceeded its goal and raised more than $1 million to fund a new wing for Quakertown Community Hospital. Johnson was a hospital board member for many years and its president from 1954 to 1971. At the campaign victory celebration, Johnson presented Million Dollar Club membership cards to all campaign workers. Inscribed on the backs of the cards was this message: "The joy of living is in the giving." Today, the hospital is known as St. Luke's Quakertown Hospital.

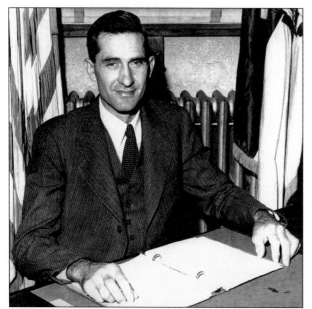

Richard E. Strayer (1910–1971) was widely respected for his dedication to the youth of Quakertown. After 17 years of teaching science, he became an assistant principal at the high school, then its principal. He was the district's superintendent from 1962 to 1971. He coached junior high basketball and the senior high rifle team, advised sophomore classes, and supervised the senior class trip. He also administered both the summer and winter recreation programs. In all these roles, he established close association with students. A few days before his death, Strayer Junior High School was dedicated to him.

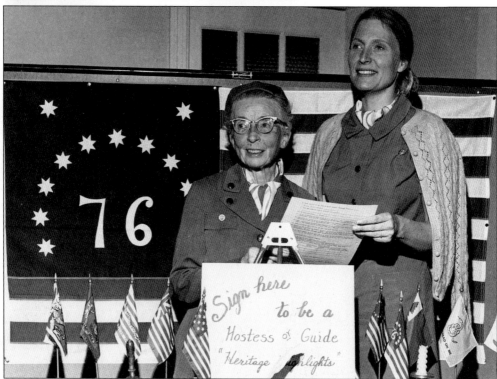

Alverna Afflerbach (1900–1990) epitomized the Girl Scout promise to serve God and country and to help others. She is on the left in this 1976 picture, helping to organize camping experiences at Camp Tohikanee. At the request of a group of girls in 1936, she formed and led Lone Star Troop I. For 54 years, she enthusiastically upheld the ideals of scouting, serving as troop leader, neighborhood chairman, troop organizer, troop consultant, and council delegate. She helped form the Bucks County Council of Girl Scouts in 1947 and assisted in the creation of Camp Tohikanee.